Praise for *Mysterious Realities*

"Story medicine is a powerful elixir in these uncertain times. Potent word-weavers like Robert Moss shape their stories in such a way that the reader feels instead of knows, journeys rather than arrives. *Mysterious Realities* offers opportunities to encounter the mystical through story without confining or defining the experience, without placing limits on what is essentially wild, ancient, and infinite." — Danielle Dulsky, E-RYT 500, YACEP, author of *The Holy Wild* and Creatrix at Living Mandala Yoga

"Robert Moss is a 'mything link,' and his new book, *Mysterious Realities*, is one of the most luminous revelations of those who travel between the worlds. Using words as wands, this magus of the imaginal realm accompanies the reader on visionary journeys, soul-capturing dreams, and encounters with once and future archetypes. This is not an innocent book. The very reading is an initiation, a sea change into something rich and strange. It is a message from a future human, a representative from a parallel world, one who has solved present challenges by entering realms that few as yet dare to enter. Read this numinous book, and enter if you dare." — Jean Houston, author of *A Mythic Life*

"What an utter delight to travel through Robert Moss's rich imaginal world. I feel like my head and heart are seven sizes bigger. What a wondrous inner adventure I've just had." — Jennifer Louden, author of *The Life Organizer* and *The Woman's Comfort Book*

"Robert Moss's *Mysterious Realities* opens doors to the worlds beyond the mundane, to the joy and grief, terror and passion of the many-branching universe. There are always more of us, following ever-deeper paths, and if we are going to find the true, the good, and the beautiful of our lives, it behooves us to explore those paths. Sink into this book and luxuriate in all that is possible — so that you, too, can cruise through your own imaginal realms." — Manda Scott, author of the Boudica Dreaming series

Praise for Other Books by Robert Moss

"Robert Moss removes the veil separating us from the underlying patterns and processes that provide meaning, direction, and joyful wonder in life.

This book is urgently needed as an antidote to the deadening chorus of materialistic science that tells us there is no purpose or direction in our world, and intention and will are illusions. *Sidewalk Oracles* is CPR for the soul."
— Larry Dossey, MD, author of *One Mind*

"Robert Moss is peerless in shifting us from seeing our life as boring and ordinary to seeing it as filled with meaningful messages and magic."
— Stephen Dinan, of The Shift Network

"The historical perspective and broad scope of meaning that Robert Moss brings to his readers are instructive — even enlightening."
— Joyce Hawkes, PhD, author of *Cell-Level Healing*

"Writing about dreams, Moss is eloquent and authoritative, a wise teacher."
— *Publishers Weekly*

"[*The Secret History of Dreaming* is] captivating, well written, and sure to please." — *Library Journal*

"*The Boy Who Died and Came Back* is a masterpiece."
— Bonnie Horrigan, author of *Red Moon Passage*

"Moss infuses the magical with the mundane in a manner that lends real weight and volume to their narratives....Believer and skeptic alike will discover that time spent with Moss will be enjoyable and perhaps life-changing." — *ForeWord*

"[*The Boy Who Died and Came Back*] by Robert Moss shares the amazing story of his life and adventures in nonordinary realms. He teaches us about dreams, the multiverse, and death and shares powerful teachings to wake us up to a new awareness of just how many paths we walk through the seen and unseen worlds." — Sandra Ingerman, MA, author of *Soul Retrieval* and *Medicine for the Earth*

"Robert Moss is a weaver of worlds. In *The Boy Who Died and Came Back*, he entwines the shamanic with the classical, the mythological with the historical with gold-threaded prose....Moss's book is a superb illustration of the restless, exuberant creativity of consciousness."
— Julia Assante, author of *The Last Frontier*

Mysterious
Realities

Mysterious Realities

A Dream Traveler's Tales from the Imaginal Realm

Robert Moss

New World Library
Novato, California

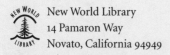
New World Library
14 Pamaron Way
Novato, California 94949

In the story "Which Is the Dream?" section 4 was first published in *Dreamgates* (© 1998, 2010) as "What to Do When You Might Be Dead in Denver."

Text design by Tona Pearce Myers

Library of Congress Cataloging-in-Publication Data
Names: Moss, Robert, [date]– author.
Title: Mysterious realities : a dream traveler's tales from the imaginal realm / Robert Moss.
Description: Novato, California : New World Library, [2018].
Identifiers: LCCN 2018020150 (print) | LCCN 2018036007 (ebook) | ISBN 9781608685394 (ebook) | ISBN 9781608685387 | ISBN 9781608685394 (ebook)
Subjects: LCSH: Dreams.
Classification: LCC BF1078 (ebook) | LCC BF1078 .M655 2018 (print) | DDC 135/.3—dc23
LC record available at https://lccn.loc.gov/2018020150

First printing, October 2018
ISBN 978-1-60868-538-7
Ebook ISBN 978-1-60868-539-4
Printed in Canada on 100% postconsumer-waste recycled paper

New World Library is proud to be a Gold Certified Environmentally Responsible Publisher. Publisher certification awarded by Green Press Initiative. www.greenpressinitiative.org

10   9   8   7   6   5   4   3   2   1

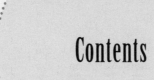

Contents

Beforetale

Under the Wings of Pegasus

Here is how this book found its way to publication. At the close of one of my workshops in Berkeley — in which synchronicity was a major theme — I walked with my coordinator to a restaurant. I talked about three things along the way. The first was Pegasus, the winged horse, born from the blood of nightmare, capable of opening the springs of the Muses — the surge of creative inspiration — under his stamping hooves. Second, I spoke of how I had many folders of "almost complete stories" that probably wanted to be put in the hands of the right publisher. I had given the collection a title long ago: *Mysterious Realities*. They were essentially just-so stories, tales from my adventures as a dreamer in many worlds. I remarked that a theme in many of these tales is that we may be living more than one life right now.

"While I am walking with you to dinner," I said to Jane by way of example, "there is another Robert who is not going out to dinner, and another who never started leading dream workshops, and another who never moved to the United States, and who knows how many Roberts who died before now."

I started talking about the many-worlds theory in physics, which holds that we are living in one of numberless parallel universes that can interact with each other. I stopped in midsentence when I saw a winged horse, white and magnificent, on the other side of the street. It was on the sign of a used bookstore: Pegasus Books.

"Excuse me," I said to Jane, "I just have to run in there."

I darted across the street, dodging cars. Fortunately Berkeley drivers are generally kind to pedestrians.

From the threshold of Pegasus Books, at eye level, I saw my surname in upper-case letters on the spine of a book. MOSS. The title of the book was *Almost Complete Poems*. I assumed the author was Howard Moss, but no, it was Stanley Moss. His poetry, previously unknown to me, was of some interest, but it was his title that seized me. I had been talking about almost complete stories, and here was an author with my surname who had actually published a collection of almost complete poems.

I looked at the book next to *Almost Complete Poems*. The title was *I Must Be Living Twice*.

Pegasus, almost complete literary productions, living parallel lives. I sensed laughter behind the curtain of the world, as if those who make these things come together were snickering, "Do you think he gets it? Is three times enough?"

I had a lunch date the next day with my favorite editor, Georgia Hughes, who had published, most recently, my book *Sidewalk Oracles*, which is all about playing with signs and synchronicity in everyday life. I had a fresh story on this theme, and I was eager to share it with her.

Synchronicity had brought Georgia and me together a decade before, and the friendship we developed had turned me, for the first time in my life, into a constant author, producing book after book on dreaming and imagination, which Georgia received with great warmth and edited with great professional insight. She is highly intuitive, and may well have picked up the fact that the creator inside me was pushing for me to deliver something different from my previous books in several genres.

We met at an Italian restaurant in Walnut Creek, California, exchanged hugs, and ordered wine. Before the wine was delivered — and before I had a chance to tell my tale of Pegasus and the almost complete stories — Georgia looked me in the eye and said, "You know what book of yours I'd like to publish next? A collection of your stories — all these amazing adventures in travel that you have in this world and the worlds where you go in your dreams."

"That's exactly what I want to do next."

I told her about my bookstore experience.

By the time our wine arrived, we had reached an agreement. We clinked glasses to celebrate the future publication of *Mysterious Realities*, with a nod to the shelf elves who were surely at play in that bookstore, under the wings of Pegasus.

Welcome to the Imaginal Realm

There is a world between time and eternity with structures created by thought that outlast anything on Earth. This is the imaginal realm. You may enter it through the gate of dreams, or the gate of death, or on nights when you drop your body like a bathrobe. Here you will find schools and palaces, places of adventure, healing, and initiation.

The imaginal realm is a fundamental ground of knowledge and experience. It is a region of mind between the world of time and the world of eternity. In this realm human imagination meets intelligences from higher realities, and they coconstruct places of healing, instruction, and initiation. Here ideas and powers beyond the grasp of the ordinary human mind — call them archetypes, tutelary spirits, gods, or daimons — take on guises humans can begin to perceive and understand.

The great medieval Sufi philosopher Suhrawardi insisted on the objective reality of the imaginal realm, and he also insisted that the way to grasp it is the way of experience: "Pilgrims of the spirit succeed in contemplating this world, and they find there every object of their desire." To know the realm of true imagi-nation, you must go there yourself. Happily for you — once you wake up to what is going on — the doors may open to you any night in dreams, or in the fertile place between sleep and waking, or in a special moment of synchronicity when the universe gets personal and you know, through your shivers, that greater powers are in play.

In dreams, we awaken to other orders of reality. When we wake up in our regular bodies, we may have fallen asleep in an-other world. Sometimes, lying in the drifty state near sleep, I sense that as I grow drowsy, a second self, back-to-back with me on the bed, is stirring awake, ready to prowl. I call him the Traveler.

I track the Traveler by recording his exploits — the ones I manage to catch — in my journal. In one report he seems to be very like my present self, just two days ahead of me, on my pres-ent probable event track. Sometimes he is much further ahead, or on a different event track, or in another body in another time or another world.

The travelers' tales in this book are just-so stories in the sense that they spring from direct experience in the imaginal realm, my own and that of other dream travelers who have shared their adventures with me. This territory is more familiar to you than you may currently realize. You are a traveler in your dreams, whether or not you remember them.

You visit realms where the dead are alive. You travel into the possible future, scouting the roads that lie ahead. You travel into the past, into scenes from your present life, and other lives that are part of your story. You go to studio sets, where dream movies are made by production crews behind the scenes, to arouse and entertain, or to shock dreamers awake. You slip into parallel lives, where your parallel selves are moving on different event tracks because they made different choices.

What is going on in your dreams doesn't necessarily stop when you wake up or switch to a different screen. The action may play on, like episodes in a television series that continue to run after you turn off the set.

It gets more interesting. When you exit a scene from a life you are leading somewhere else, you may or may not remember where you were and who you are in that other world. When you do remember, you tag what lingers in your mind as a dream.

When you exit a dream that is also a visit to a parallel life, your parallel self continues on its way. While you go about your day, your other self may dream of you.

In *Mysterious Realities*, you'll confirm that the doors to the imaginal realm open from wherever you are. You'll see what it means to live on a mythic edge. At any moment, you may fall, like the author, into the lap of a goddess or the jaws of an archetype. Are you ready? A survival tip: don't go to any world without your sense of humor.

A Storytelling of Crows

Airport security is easy this evening. I breeze through the pre-check line without having to take off my shoes or my belt. Belle and Annie want to shop for presents — someone's birthday is coming up — so I tell them I'll scout for a pub on our concourse and meet them there. A pub that I like, where you can sit outside in a pretend beer garden and people-watch, is at the far end of the concourse, but it has closed early. Reluctantly, I turn around and walk back, toward a pub with an African theme that I like less.

I pause at the newsstand to get a bottle of water. I don't expect much in the way of books in a shop like this, but they have an extensive display that includes a rack of Penguin Classics. I glance at authors and titles. Guy de Maupassant, E. M. Forster, Dostoyevsky. There's a story collection by a writer unknown to me with a really creepy title: *Songs of a Dead Dreamer*. The cover illustration is even creepier. The figure staring out at the viewer looks like one of the evil dead. I have to buy the book, if only to joke about the title with the girls when they catch up with me.

Book in hand, bottled water in the side of my carry-on, I head for the fake African pub.

Then my right foot goes sliding, followed by my left, and I am airborne. I don't understand how I slipped. I tell myself to let my body go slack, hoping to escape broken bones when I come down on the hard surface of the walkway. I have the odd sensation that I am hovering, that something is keeping me up. People moving around me are blurry, frames in a slideshow that isn't paused. Yet I am paused, at nine on a Friday evening, in an airport I thought I knew well, but not like this.

From my horizontal position, I see a pair of horrible yellow curly-toed pumps, brothel-creepers from an Eastern harem. They can only belong to Ali. I see his narrow, oily face leering down at me. His eyes are masked by wrap-around sunglasses.

"He wants you," says Ali. "Come on."

I get up as if I am getting out of bed. I have the feeling I'm leaving something behind. I would like to look, but I'm being moved too fast. I still have *Songs of a Dead Dreamer* in my hand.

I say to Ali, "Why are you wearing shades?"

"We are among the shades."

The scene has shifted. Through a forest choked with vines and creepers, I see a black mountain ahead. This is not the way I wish to see *him*. Hot tongues of flame flash in and out of the moving mountain. Black limbs flourish weapons. There are eyes, bulging, reddened, uncountable tusks and teeth. And a cavernous opening in the belly of the mountain that gives the impression of an organic meat grinder.

"He is not in a good mood," Ali says, unnecessarily. He prostrates himself before the living mountain.

I can't move my gaze from what is moving inside that cavernous opening. It reminds me now of the mechanism of an immense and complicated clock. Are those human figures, bound to its moving parts in their revolutions?

Through the hiss of steam and the crackle of fire, I hear a softer, subtler sound coming from the mountain. No question. It is the ticking of a clock.

"Please show yourself as you did before," I say to the mountain. "In a form in which I can bear to look at you."

I remain standing. Prostration is not my thing. Nor are titles and praise names. But I do add, "Great one." This seems good policy.

A blast of hot air sears my skin. A great maddened eye glares into mine. Giant arms or pincers are raised above me.

"I have a story," I pant, trying not to buckle. "I think you will like it."

The forward movement of the monstrous mountain slows.

"Is it about me?"

He is changed. He has assumed the appearance I can deal with best. He looks like a maharaja in beautifully tailored clothes, speaking English with an Oxbridge accent.

"Of course." This was not an exact truth. I would need to write him in.

"Then begin."

I recite from memory:

The smell of crushed shellfish was strongest around dawn. The dye makers kept their laborers up all night, grinding to make purple for the robes of emperors and the hems of senators.

The centurion groaned and sniffed. He would never like the smell of this Phoenician city.

His mistress draped her long body over his and murmured in his ear, "I dreamed of the Galilean again."

The centurion groaned louder and reached for the beaker of wine he had left near the bed. He was surrounded by talk of the Jew who was said to have vanished from the cave where he was buried. The centurion was all but certain that his followers had spirited the corpse away to manufacture a miracle, to turn a low rabble-rouser into a *theos aner*, a god-man of the old style.

Still, his woman had the sight. And Phoenician witches were good with dreams. Everyone said so.

"Enough!" Yama has shapeshifted again. He is now seated in a director's chair, wearing expensive but garish clothes with conflicting patterns, and smoking a very large cigar.

"Enough with that old story. I'm sick of it. Besides, the movie has already been made."

"What movie?"

"The one where a Roman officer plays detective, investigating the disappearance of Jesus's body. You took too long to finish that story. When you don't nail down a story as a script or a book, it flies away from you to be told by someone else. Don't you understand that yet?"

This is dismaying news. I thought my story of the centurion and the Phoenician witch was a winner.

"Besides, we processed Cornelius ages ago." He snaps his fingers for his recorders. How does he know the name I have given to my fictional centurion? Oh, right, he would know.

"What happened to Cornelius the Illyrian?" Yama snaps at one of his clerks.

"He was sent to a different department. Through the Gate of Horn."

"Let's get to the point." Yama is stirring and swelling, massing again as that smoking black mountain. "We have to talk about your life situation."

"I'm happy to talk," I say with no conviction.

"I am glad to hear that, my dear. But your situation is such that I can only talk with you if you wear my noose around your neck."

"I accept."

With the thought, it is there. Yama's necktie. The noose with which he takes souls out of bodies. I feel its brush against my throat, but he lets it hang loosely, flopping down over my collarbones.

"Before we continue our conversation," the Death Lord tells me, "you will talk with my Recorders."

There they are, with their registers. They remind me of intelligent, hairless chimpanzees. Long fingers turning pages. So many names and details. Haven't they upgraded their technology since the Raj?

"What is this about?" I dare to ask. I think I know the answer, but I would like to move things along.

"There are three exit ramps in plain sight," one of them tells me. He gives me a date two years into the future.

"How?"

"Death by choking."

Okay, a useful reminder. I make a mental note to chew my food properly, especially when the food is a warm, crusty baguette, and to remember that time frame. I reach for a pen to write it down, then realize that writing here won't do me any good, as in one of those dreams where you think you are writing your dream in a journal and wake to find the page is blank.

"The next exit date," Yama's clerk continues. This is a further two years into the future. Nothing to worry about now. But I want to know how.

"Death by drowning."

So, in this scenario, I stroke out. I smile at my lousy mental pun. I will myself to hold the memory of that day, four years into the future, when I could die by water.

I am ready to hear my third exit date. I assume this will take me out to my maximum allotment of time in this life. That is how things are supposed to work.

"No point in thinking about that, my dear." It is Yama himself who is speaking. "Tell him."

"Today is the day. The time of your death is now."

Now? But I'm not ready. I feel a stab of grief. I see the faces of those I love, of those who love me. We have so much more life to share. I think of things I have left undone, of seas where I never swam, of flowers I never smelled, of books I left unwritten.

"It can't be now," I protest.

"The probability that you will depart your body now is 98 percent," says the clerk, talking as if he has an unseen calculator. "It will reach 100 percent when Belle accepts the fifty pounds of kayla."

"Fifty pounds of *what*? What is kayla?"

The Recorder runs a thin finger down his nose. He does not explain.

"You once said it was your practice to be ready to leave your body whenever I came for you." Again it is the voice of the master. I feel the noose tighten around my neck. It no longer feels silky. It feels like nylon coated with powdered glass, like manja string.

Hmmm. Yes, I did say that, didn't I? I am confused now. I left my body somewhere — oh yes, at Seattle airport — in midair.

One of Yama's eyes expands until it becomes a television screen. Looking into it, I see my broken body being lifted onto a stretcher. It is carried back through the concourse. Belle and Annie are running after it, sobbing. Someone has given them my stuff. Annie grimaces at the cover of *Songs of a Dead Dreamer*. My body is loaded into the back of an ambulance. A paramedic is performing CPR. Heads are shaking. The heart has stopped. Is this the end of this body, on the exit ramp from an airport?

"I want a deal," I tell Yama. His shape is not steady. It flickers between the perfumed maharaja in his peacock finery and the smoking black mountain.

"You have nothing to deal with," he tells me.

"I have a story. That has always counted for you."

He considers this. I know he is sensitive to the fact that he is missing from so many of the myths and legends that are woven around other members of the pantheon. The masters who wrote the Katha Upanishad did him honor, making him an ultimate spiritual teacher for the one who is willing to step through his fire. But that is a rare exception.

"No centurion. No messiah," he specifies.

"Agreed."

"I am listening." Now he is reclining on a divan, fanned by handmaidens beating peacock plumes.

I tell him a story that begins where I left my body. In this version, I do not die in the ambulance. So the story is also an essay in parallel realities. I tell it like this:

I am flat on my back on the hard floor of the airport concourse. There are concerned faces above me. One man wants to know if he should call an ambulance. It was such a hard fall that something must be broken.

As they help me to my feet, I reassure them I am fine. Truly I am. I don't understand why I am feeling no pain. It is as if some giant hand carried me down, like an air mattress. Someone hands me the horror book.

I see people rushing to put some orange witches' hats around the slick of liquid that caused my spill.

"I guess I should be more careful about my in-flight reading," I joke to the girls when we meet at the pizza joint, the only place still open where we can get a beer. I want to ask Belle a strange

question, about fifty pounds of kayla, whatever that is, but I sense
that this might take me into a story I don't want to play out. The
ladies are off to other places, so I board my plane alone. They have
me up against a bulkhead on the aisle, so I can stretch my leg but
must pull in my shoulders — they are very broad — every time a
flight attendant comes by with a cart.

I might manage a nap tonight, I think. I open *Songs of a Dead
Dreamer* at random and find myself in the midst of a story about
a dummy in a shop window who dreams of being human, or vice
versa. I don't think I'll go there for now.

The seats beside me are empty. Maybe I'll be able to stretch
out. An extraordinary figure is coming down the aisle. She seems
immensely tall, with her high-heeled boots and top hat. She is
wearing black leather over a bustier. She points at the seat next to
me. I stand to let her in. She turns to a short, pudgy man behind
her, directing him to take the window seat.

As we buckle up, I notice her gloves. The fingers are cut out.
On the backs are huge death's heads.

I'm usually game to chance an encounter with strangers on
airplanes. It's really an ideal situation to taste other people's life
stories without any commitment beyond the duration of the
flight. However, I have four hours ahead, and I'm not sure where
conversation with the lady with the death's-head gloves may lead.

She breaks the ice when we start taxiing out onto the run-
way. She turns around, inspects the cabin, and declares, "I like
this flight."

When I glance her way, she goes on, "All the seats are taken.
Actuarially, when a plane is going to crash, at least 20 percent of
the seats are empty."

Her male companion is leaning against the window, snoring
gently.

"You look like a magician," I tell the lady.

"I do commit magic, in a way."

"In any special way?"

"Let's just say that spankings are my friends."

If I have understood correctly, she has just announced her occupation. She is a dominatrix. Not my scene. I hastily hide my horror book with the horrible cover behind an airline magazine.

Conversation lapses until the cart comes round. She wants crème de menthe, which they don't have. She settles for vodka, double.

She sips and plays with a long braid of hair falling from under the brim of her hat.

"Do you think the dead come to us in dreams?" she asks brightly, out of silence.

"Absolutely." I don't hesitate.

"Oh, good. My dead husband showed up at my bedside last night. He was a rock musician. He was shot in the face in a diner last year. It was in the papers. Anyway, he said he came to tell me that he's doing okay. He's got a new job doing music and special effects for dreams that are being produced where he is. Then the dreams are played in the minds of people down here. What do you think of that?"

"I think it's a good story."

She sniffs and takes another swig of vodka, and silence falls between us again. The cabin lights are dimmed. Most of the passengers are napping or watching videos.

The dominatrix leans against me. "Are you awake?"

"Uh-huh." I open my eyes.

"You're a writer, aren't you?"

"I put together a few tales."

"I've got an idea for you."

My Life as a Dominatrix. A succession of possible titles streams through my mind. *A Story That Will Pierce You.* I assume that she thinks her life story is worth a book. Doesn't everyone?

She snuggles next to me, sucking on that loose braid of ginger hair. She puts her mouth right up against my ear. I can feel her warm breath. She murmurs, "I'd love to read a story told from the point of view of Jezebel."

I am trying to remember the Bible account of Jezebel.

She puts her hand on my thigh. "Those Phoenician witches are so good with dreams."

I pull away, stunned. She knows a story I have been working on. How is that possible? Is her dead husband — the one she said is doing special effects for dreams — speaking in her mind?

I stammer something tepid, like, "It's an interesting idea." And pretend to sleep.

When I open my eyelids, the cabin is even darker than before, and one of my legs remains asleep until I hobble back to the restroom. I pick up a beer from the galley before returning to my seat.

As soon as I reclaim my seat, her eyes are on me. As before, her words come gusting out of nowhere, like the erratic winds of the Midi.

"I like crows. And ravens," she announces.

"Of course you do."

"Do you know the collective noun for a group of crows or ravens?"

Ah. A chance to gain a few points in this staccato conversation. I am quite proud of myself when I respond, "Yes, I do. It is a murder of crows, and an *unkindness* of ravens." I am theatrical as I say *unkindness.* It has always seemed to me even more sinister than *murder.*

"Oh, everyone knows *that,*" she counters, dismissive to the point of spitting. "There is another word, far more interesting, and it applies both to crows and ravens. Do you want to know what it is?"

"Okay."

"It is a *storytelling*. Of crows, or of ravens. Would you like to know why that term fits *precisely*?"

"I am sure you are going to tell me."

"I saw this myself. I came upon a large gathering of crows — a *storytelling*. They were silent, except for one crow at the center who was talking away. Crows have quite a large vocabulary, you know. He cawed and he squalled and he clacked and he shook out his feathers. He was obviously telling a story. But he was a defective storyteller. When he finished his story, they pecked him to death."

I clench my fists and sit very still.

"What do you think of that?"

"It's a good story," I croak.

Silence falls between us again until we are on the ground. The dozy man by the window rouses himself now. The dominatrix introduces us, though she has not confided her own name. "This is Homer, my chaperone."

"Have a good odyssey, Homer," I say, shaking his hand.

"All I want is a bowling alley," Homer says, his speech slightly slurred.

"A bowling alley?" I'm not sure I heard him correctly.

"Yep. A one-lane bowling alley."

"A one-lane bowling alley," I echo him again.

"You bet. Something to do when you get *old*."

I find this as creepy as the image of the storytelling of crows pecking an unsatisfactory storyteller to death.

I stretch my legs, and my back. I find the usual creaks and complaints after hours of sitting in an airplane seat, but no trace of my fall at the airport. Did it really happen? Was I hurled far enough from my body to meet Death in his own realm? How did I come down safely?

I remember Homer's account of Priam crossing safely through the enemy lines at night because the hand of a god was held over him.

What power placed its hand under me, on that airport concourse?

I smell chicken blood, and other fluids. In that instant, I am sitting on a woven mat in a room full of images, carved from wood, wrought from iron. The lean black man in front of me is casting a set of bronze medallions for me. He is asking, *¿Quién te defiende ante las orishas?*

That is always the question, in any world. Who supports you among the greater powers? In the Yoruba tradition, they are called *orishas*. Others call them *gods* or *devas* or *neteru* or *archetypes*. Their forms are never fixed, despite human efforts to hold them to patterns so your head doesn't explode when you begin to see them in their larger identities. Arjuna asked to see Krishna in his cosmic form and then couldn't deal with what he was shown: the birth and the death of worlds. I see again the world-devouring clock, the cosmic meat grinder, in Yama's belly.

Well, I have been reminded of my assignment. I will be allowed to live as long as I keep generating stories that entertain Death. How do I explain this to my agent?

"It's about entertainment, kid." Marty winks at me.

He picks up a shopping bag that is leaning on the desk and places it on top. The label is from a Beverly Hills store. "Look at this," he removes a note from inside and waves it at me so I can see the letterhead, with the name of a bestselling author. She has signed the note in coral red lipstick.

Now he pulls out a mess of pages and riffles through them, showing me sketches written on napkins and notes, inviting editors to fill in the blanks.

"They'll take it, and they'll pay what we want, because she entertains. It doesn't matter whether she can write a grammatical sentence. What matters is what keeps people turning the pages. Sure, this is hen lit. But it's women who buy most of the fiction. Speaking of which, where are your female characters? If you're going soft on me, you'd better produce a hard-on for the ladies you want to read you."

He plays with an unlit cigar. He was nicer when he could smoke at the office.

"I do know it's about entertainment." I meet Marty's point of view, short of the Beverly Hills shopping bag. I don't tell him that entertainment is a life-or-death matter for me right now.

I'm thinking about women characters.

I have one. I must allow Lorelei to tell her story in her own voice. I trust this will dissuade Yama from tightening his necktie around my throat.

The Lost Girl
and the Fairy
of the Copper Beech

You are about to enter a modern fairy tale. It is a true story, told in the voice of a woman who found, to her amazement, that her beautiful lost girl — the one who went missing when a dream of romance was crushed — had been held safe among the roots of a special tree in the place where she was first kissed. Like life, the tale is still unfolding. To reclaim our lost girls and boys, we must prove to them that we are safe and we are fun. Listen to Lorelei tell her story, and consider how much of it is about you.

I went to my favorite used bookshop in Vienna after I heard you say in an interview that we need to find the bigger story of our lives. I stopped for angel's kisses — my favorite cookies — at the bakery along the street. I was afraid that the bookshop might have closed, because I had not been there since I was quite young. But it was still open, and Herr Müller was still there behind the counter, a little balder and thinner than when I last saw him, surrounded by cats, with a bilingual edition of Dante in his hands.

"*Ma tu, perche vai?*" he greeted me in fourteenth-century Tuscan. Before I had figured it out, he translated for me, "But you, why are you traveling?"

"I have come looking for the bigger story of my life."

"Ah. For that, you must go in the back room."

I knew this was a privilege. The back room was reserved for rare volumes kept in locked cabinets, and for boxes of books Herr Müller had recently purchased that had not yet been priced and sorted.

"Keep your intention in mind, and don't expect anything in particular." He dropped his voice. "That room is full of shelf elves, and more."

This strange reception brought a flutter of hope. My life had been drab in recent years. It was often hard for me to get out of bed in the morning. I don't know how I would have managed without the discipline of a steady job and decent workmates. There was no man who was important in my life, and when I was honest with myself, I had to admit that love had been missing since my heart was broken when I was fourteen. Going out with girlfriends for a few glasses of wine or a movie and sometimes dancing with strangers — usually avoiding anything beyond the dance — were my prime amusements.

As I threaded my way through towers of books into the back room, I wondered what would leap out at me.

I was struck by the beauty of the bindings of the books in the cases against the wall to my right. I saw intricate patterns of foliage and vines, traced in gold leaf on rich green and brown covers. Was that an early edition of *The Golden Bough*? Was that a complete set of the Color Fairy books? Either series would be a likely place to find a story.

I turned my head away and thrust out an arm to pluck a book

at random from one of the shelves. I felt something give. My hand closed on something moist and springy. I turned to look and found I was holding a little branch, the branch of an apple tree. The wall of books had been drawn away, like a curtain. I stepped forward, amazed, into an apple orchard.

It was lovely here, under dappled light. I wondered if I was meant to eat one of the apples. Wasn't that the way that people traveled to the Otherworld in some of the fairy stories? I chose a little apple that was more golden than red, but found it tart, and let it fall after a single bite. It did not seem to have had any effect.

But I saw now that beyond the apple orchard and some patches of wildflowers, there were deeper woods. I felt called to follow the path that wound into the forest.

I looked over my shoulder a few times to make certain I could see the way back.

Something hit me on the shoulder. I looked down and saw a little stick, with some carved symbols on it that made me think of runes.

I looked up, and a large black bird cawed at me from the high branches of a tree.

I took another step, and I was struck again, by another piece of wood with similar markings. I looked up at the tree and saw a man in a hooded robe where the bird had been. His robe seemed to be made of black feathers.

"What are you doing in my wood?" the man in the tree growled at me.

I told him *you* had sent me.

"Why?" he demanded.

"I was told I need to find the bigger story of my life."

He pulled on his beard, considering this. I decided, in that moment, that I must be talking to a druid.

"I have a story for you." He cocked his head. "There is another tree, far from here. It is the kind you call a copper beech. Do you remember it?"

Of course. It was a tree I had known since early childhood. It stands in a park in Vienna. It was under that tree that I found and lost the love of my life.

"There is a fairy in that tree," the druid went on. "She has been holding a part of your soul safe for many years. It is time for you to go to her and see whether you can get your lost girl back."

"But how can I do that?"

"Ask the one who sent you here."

I sought guidance from *you*. Do you remember what you said? You told me a wild old Celtic fairy story, where men turn into sows and flowers turn into lovely girls, and it came to the part where someone with a storied name *sings* a beloved kinsman out of a tree, where he is hanging like rotten fruit. You said, "You need the right song to bring to the copper beech. Go to the tree the druid told you about when you have found it."

I went back to the bookshop, but the back room did not open into an orchard and a forest.

I cried for further guidance, and in the hour before dawn a blackbird came and perched on my windowsill. It seemed to me that it said, "When you go to the beech tree, dress pretty. Wear high heels, put on your sexiest dress. You want to look like you are ready to have some fun, and are fun to be around. Take gifts for the tree, and the tree fairy. Expect the unexpected."

I went back to my birth city. I still did not have a song. I cried for a song.

I dreamed I was on a boat train, walking hand in hand with Paul McCartney.

The dream had no soundtrack, but when I came back from it I thought that the song I needed must be from the Beatles. I asked myself what was my favorite Beatles song, going back to when I was fourteen.

It came lilting and swaying through my mind.

Something in the way she moves…

I was fourteen again, and Kurt was singing that to me off-key, dancing with me in the park, holding me close. He kissed me under the copper beech that day, and I would have let him do anything. My body was a mass of nerve endings, quivering with delight. Then the tolling of a bell cut through the music of my senses. It was just the bell of the monastery church near the park, sounding an Angelus, as it always did at that time of day. But with it I felt my father's hands on my throat, his heavy bulk pressing the air from my lungs.

Kurt and I had so little time before our love was detected and we were forced apart.

I knew exactly when and why a beautiful part of me — that lovely teen with her blend of innocence and sensual longing — had left me then.

Through my tears, I let the old Beatles tune play in my mind until the words slipped away and I had only the music. It would not be enough to take a borrowed song. I could take the melody, but I must refurbish it with words of my own, in my own language.

The words came to me. I wrote them in the big looping letters I wrote in school composition books, but on scented pink paper. I was ready to go to the copper beech.

I put on a black strapless dress I hadn't worn in years. It still fitted me well enough, and showed the right amount of curves. I had purchased some new heels for this occasion, with a price tag that would have made me run away under other circumstances. I made some little bows with pink ribbons, not sure what gifts to bring to a copper beech and a tree fairy.

In the park, I walked round the tree three times — they say that three times makes the charm — singing my version of the Beatles song. I got nothing in return, except deepening sadness out of memory.

I tied my ribbon bows to the lower branches of the trees, hoping that no park attendant would come to accuse me of littering or worse. Nothing happened.

I heard the tolling of the bells of the monastery church, and fled.

The whole enterprise was crazy, something out of the kind of storybook my father told me bred superstition and ignorance. I went back to the bakery for cappuccino and angel's kisses, and looked at the train timetable. I could catch an evening train back to the city where I now live and work, in border country.

Yet as dusk settled, I was back in the park, sitting on the bench in front of the copper beech. I sang my song again.

I heard laughter and thumping from the children's playground.

I closed my eyes. The din of the children was oddly relaxing. Instead of feeling irritated or distracted, I felt myself being carried to a deeper space. The laughter and the pounding feet were like the beat of a drum.

I saw a cave opening among the roots of the beech, which slithered like snakes. I was a little afraid of them, but willed myself to go through, and down.

I found a beautiful girl. Her hair was in braids. I haven't worn those since my early teens. She was so lovely. She seemed to be sleeping. Then I noticed that she was bound. More of those tree roots, and rhizomes, were wrapped around her.

I looked again, and saw that it was not tree roots that were restraining her. She was in the grip of a being with a puzzling anatomy, more tree than humanoid, with great translucent wings that might have been borrowed from a butterfly.

"Lorelei?" I spoke to my younger self.

She opened her eyes and looked at me. She frowned, clearly puzzled.

"I've missed you. I want us to be together," I said.

"Who are you?"

"You know who I am, sweetie. You've dreamed of me. If you come with me, we'll have fun and you'll always be safe, I promise."

"Will you take me dancing?"

"Of course!"

"Can I sing with you?"

"As much as you like."

"Will you paint again, and let me pick the colors?"

"You will choose what we paint."

"Can I have some of those angel's kisses?"

"We'll go to the bakery and get a double order."

She was standing up now, released from the tendrils of the tree fairy. I put out my arms to her. It felt so good to hold me.

Excuse me. The interruption came with cold shivers. How can I describe the expression I found in the strange eyes of the tree fairy when I made myself look? Obdurate, that's the word that comes. *She is ours more than yours. She will never wholly belong to you. I will let you take her out, but she will come here before dawn every day to be with me. Because, whatever you say, you are not safe, and your life is not balanced.*

Through my tears, I knew the tree fairy was right. I am not safe. But I can be fun. I took my lovely girl by the hand, to show her the bows I had tied to the tree.

As we circled the trunk, I noticed initials carved on the trunk, inside a heart. L and K, like Lorelei and Kurt. I am certain they were not there before.

"Can we get angel's kisses now?" my girl asked me.

"Of course."

I am recording this now in my red book, a journal bound in leather the color of the copper beech in its glory of fall foliage. I will write every day, and I will close the red book with a clasp and a key. My lovely girl was never permitted to have personal space, even within the covers of a journal. As I grow the contents of the red book, I hope that the space of us will grow large enough, and safe enough, to persuade the tree fairy to let her stay with me all the time.

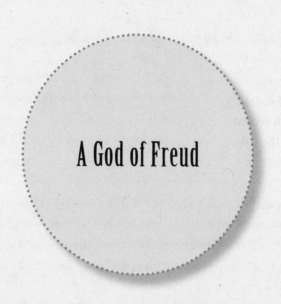

A God of Freud

Before I visited Freud's last home in Hampstead in 2011, nothing I had read had prepared me for the amazing sight of the army of gods and sacred beings in the study. There, on his desk, was a head of Osiris that he called the *Answerer*. Here was Isis, rather formally posed as she suckled her child, a queenly and hieratic mother. Here were falcon-headed gods like the ones he saw in a childhood dream, carrying his mother to the gates of the netherworld.

In life, Freud was reluctant to go anywhere without a selection of his "old and grubby gods" in attendance. He was forever talking to his little gods, stroking them, handling them, handing one to a patient, or placing one between himself and a difficult case. He knew that the ancients regarded these statues as breathing images, that some part of a deity or daimon had been called into each one. Nothing in his collection (except the fakes that escaped detection by his keen eye and those of his friends at the Kulturhistorisches Museum in Vienna) was made simply

for the sake of art and ornament. They were very much alive
for him.

You are about to enter Dr. Freud's world of dreams and
statue magic. You may discover something about how gods
are made.

1

It is the dream. Watched by the dealer, he handles the piece carefully. He closes his hand around it. The statuette is slightly warm
to the touch. The skin is reddish ochre, the paint chipped just a
little. White kilt. The headdress just a fringe hanging down below
the raptor head with its cruel beak.

He pats the contours like a blind man. He is certain. This was
one of the falcon men he watched carry his mother through the
gates of Death. *Take me.* There is a glow in the jeweled eyes, like
fire under ash.

The price the dealer demands is exorbitant, even by the stan-
dards of Vienna's exhibitionistic rich. The dealer observes, without apology, that there are always eager customers for a Horus
of this quality. The Lichtensteins, for example. Surely the Herr
Doktor knows their collection? But of course. Only the previous
week he had been at the palace during the hours it was open to a
select public, after the hour he reserves for patients without ap-
pointments.

Horus. The avenger of the father, the one who tramples on
snakes and scorpions, whose amulets guard against sorcery and
heal the sick. Horus of the King's Touch. The one who walked
with his mother to the gates of the afterlife.

He will take the piece. No, Herr Lustig, I will bring it home
myself. No elaborate wrapping. Perhaps a cloth, like a mummy
bandage, to keep it safe in my pocket.

He avoids the brownshirts in the streets. There have always been Jew haters in Austria. This, too, we will survive.

At home, Martha is resigned to the addition of one more ancient figure to his collection. She has said they belong in a museum, to which he has made the obvious response: "My consulting rooms *are* a museum." Only he knows how many old and grubby gods these rooms contain. He did not complete his last inventory. The number of objects had climbed above two thousand before he gave up on the count.

He places the falcon-headed god on his desk and checks on the reactions of the other idols that crowd the space — austere Osiris, fat-bellied Buddha, Athena straight as a spear, a randy satyr, an Eros rising from his lover's bed, a deep-bosomed earth goddess.

He strokes and caresses, testing responses, some harsh, some affectionate, some signaling the urgent need to be fed or walked. He called himself a godless Jew, yet he goes nowhere without his battalions of gods.

Gripping the new and ancient god with the raptor's beak, he intones the words a baleful Mother of the Gods used to raise the most terrible of the Furies against an errant hero:

Flectere si nequeo superos, Acheronta movebo.
If I cannot bend the higher gods, I will move the infernal
    regions.

2

He wakes irritable and in pain. He feels that some Fury has inserted cold iron into his lower jaw and is jabbing and rattling it. He sees his head as a skull, with the jawbone hanging loose, in an awful parody of laughing Death.

He must catch the dream. He is making his rounds of wealthy clients in their grand apartments and palazzos around the Ringstrasse. They greet him with the usual formality but with evident confusion. They tell him, sometimes over tea and cake, sometimes at the door, that his colleague came around shortly before.

What colleague? The name sounds like "Heid." What treatment did this Doctor Heid provide? The answers are maddeningly vague. It seems that this interloper attempted some version of the talking cure, goading his patients to relate their dreams and fantasies, then expounding his own theories with thundering certainty, but in such a gassy and obscure fashion that no one could reproduce his exact opinions. Were these patients satisfied? Well, they had no doubt that Heid was a great doctor. They made it clear they had no need of the Herr Doktor Professor's services that day.

In his velvet smoking jacket, he carries these shards from his dream into his consulting room. While the family rooms are furnished in dowdy bourgeois taste, the room he shares with his books and his patients — and his battalions of gods — is laid out in oriental splendor. At his desk, he lights a cigar, and lets the tobacco ease the pain in his jaw. He strokes a winged phallus from a Roman villa, wishing for the perennial virility it suggests. He kisses the brow of Athena. He pats the back of the fat green jade toad. His eye, then his fingers, stray to the newcomer among his miniature gods and daimons. In his dream of his mother's death, the falcon-headed god was a walker with the departed. Therefore a traveler.

Can you show me Doctor Heid? Will you take me to what I need to see?

He leaves the cigar unfinished and reclines on his sofa, which offers the splendid view of a garden in paradise — the design of the Qashqai rug he placed over it years ago, to the amazement of the patients he has invited to lie there and tell their dreams, amid a grander and more exotic dream.

His aim is to find the vanishing — or hidden — quack from his own dream. Always alert for rhymes and puns, he notes that *Heid* sounds like the English word *hide*. To hide is to conceal oneself. As a noun, a hide may be a place of concealment, like the shelter in which the hunter waits for the deer to break cover. He remembers, also from the English, another "Hyde" in a story of doubles of profound psychological interest, on which he intends to write a paper. Then there is a line from Heraclitus. Something about how nature *hides*.

With the falcon-man in his hand, an untested talisman, he lets himself drift toward dream, on the Qashqai garden. And finds himself in one of his sepia dreams. Everything is brownish-gray, as in the photographs of the Roman Forum he has on his walls. But the scene is of a region he has never visited in his physical body. It appears to be in the South Pacific, among islands of waving palms and bright waterfalls and alluring, dark-skinned women. There is a sensual beauty about the whole scene. He notices below him, on the gentle waves, the shadow of wings. He wants to swoop down and enter the lives of the island people.

Instead he is required to watch the movements of a warship sailing among the islands of this tropical nirvana. He is certain the ship is German; something tells him it is a minesweeper. On the captain's bridge, he sees a man in civilian clothes — short jacket, riding pants, puttees. He is tall and stocky, with the air of a Junker or perhaps a tough peasant farmer. Can this be Doctor Heid?

The minesweeper is doing its work. The crewmen are dropping depth charges in metal barrels into the azure waters. As the explosives burst, far below, things from the depths are blown to the surface. The islanders are wailing and mourning, because the sea and the beaches are covered with blood and muck, with mangled carcasses, with horrible misshapen things no one has seen or named before.

The dreamer stirs, doubly in pain again. Has he been shown the effect of depth psychology? Is this what happens when you blow away the layers of repression and denial and get to the primal horror in a life?

He realizes, with relief, that the figure on the captain's bridge, who can only be Doctor Heid, is familiar. He strongly resembles his lost protégé, Carl Jung, who is built like a strapping Swiss hay cutter. So this is about Jung as a competitor, and the explosive and unhelpful consequences of his method. It occurs to him that Doctor Heid may be his double, his Mr. Hyde, the one he prefers not to see, and that his identification of this disastrous doctor with another person may be an example of his own theory of wish fulfillment. But he blows these uncomfortable thoughts away when he lights a fresh cigar.

He pets the little falcon god. Thank you for your company. He wonders where they will go together next time.

3

He stands under the leafless arms of the almond tree in the front garden. He is here to die. Under their umbrellas, people look at him quickly as they hurry down Maresfield Gardens to the steep path down to the high-street buses. What do they see? An old man — a foreigner, a Jew — in a homburg hat, with a ragged gray beard that fails to conceal a wound. To think that he once had a fine dark beard worthy of a conquistador, and had it trimmed by a barber every day, even on the day of his father's funeral!

He shivers in the cold London rain, remembering last night's dream. His father, Jacob, came to his bedside, looking amazingly young and prosperous. He announced he had come to take Sigmund on a journey. "But how can I travel?" Freud protested. "I am very ill, and so tired." "Don't worry about that. You will travel light, in your body of air. Like me." Astonished and incredulous, he allowed his father to guide him. By ways he could not now recall, they had arrived at the Forum in Rome, in front of the little temple of Minerva a barbaric pope had ordered broken down and destroyed. But now the temple was restored. The goddess stood with her spear — straight as Athena, her Greek sister or original. He offered her a prayer. "Lady of Wisdom, you who restrained the Furies, have the infernal powers kindly return whence they came."

Anna is in the garden, urging him to take something for breakfast. He must find the strength to record his dream in detail. It was a fine example of his theory of wish fulfillment. He wished that his father had been handsome and successful. He wished that Jacob was still alive. He wished that the temple of Minerva had never been destroyed. He wished there were friendly gods who could hear the call of humans in a time of pain and fear.

He takes only tea, and the drug. He sits at the desk in his consulting room, with a shawl over his knees, among his gods. Dreaming of the dead, feeling Death in the room, he has added another memento mori to the plunder of the tomb robbers. It is a Roman urn of green-gold blown glass. Through the unstoppered neck, he can sniff the semen smell of burned bones. The funerary urn came complete with the shards of burned bone that remained after the ashes from cremation had long since blown away. Burned bones. He had read somewhere in his archaeology and anthropology books that this was a name for an aspect of the dead that stayed close to the living after death, hungry and jealous.

If I am burned, he speaks to the bones, I want to be burned thoroughly. I want nothing of this broken and stinking body, gangrenous and riddled with cancer, to survive. Then I will be released to become soil, or motes on a west wind.

But what if there is more? All the cultures that produced his little gods and *shabtis* believed there is something of a man — soul or atman, *ba* or psyche — that survives the death of the body. They thought a part of psyche might take up residence in a statue or a mummified body or another soul-house after death, while another part flies free, on roads of another world.

His eyes, then his hands, move to the falcon-headed god. He addresses it with his mind: you are alive. As all of you are, he adds, surveying his legions. But you — he returns to Horus — have a special life and a special vocation. You are the one who kept me safe, and got all of us here, through the Gestapo and the bullyboys who have possessed my country.

Anna is at the door. He has a visitor. He remembers now that he agreed to let an antiques dealer from Bond Street call on him. He no longer sees patients, but he has not altogether given up collecting. It has taken the place of sex. It is his way of asserting his manhood, of rallying his ruined body to take command.

He has agreed with himself that at this point in his life he will only purchase new items if he can release one as full or partial trade. His visitor, Mr. Oliver, has some interesting jewels — carnelian intaglios like the head of Jupiter he wears in a gold ring on the fourth finger of his right hand; Baltic amber; an obsidian mirror. Freud makes his selection and proposes a trade. Mr. Oliver is interested in the falcon-headed god on the desk.

Freud tells him, a little sharply, that this is not available. Nonetheless, he allows the dealer to handle the piece. Mr. Oliver inspects the base and frowns. "Very well," he says quickly, handing the figure back.

Puzzled, Freud asks his visitor's opinion.

"I'm sorry to say that the piece is a forgery. No older than Champollion. I would guess nineteenth century, actually."

Freud is outraged. He asks the dealer to show him. Mr. Oliver points to the incriminating signs. How could Lustig, Vienna's foremost dealer in such antiquities, have missed them? How could Freud himself, with his keen and developing instinct for such things, have been duped?

"Whatever you say," he tells the dealer, "this figure is real." In his mind, he adds, *I have made it real*. This is how gods are made.

At the Moon Café

Have you ever walked the path of moonlight on water?

Diana loves the beach best like this, the sand shining white in the moonlight, driftwood rising to form the rib cages of ancient beasts, the wing bones of giant birds. The summer people and the surfers are gone, leaving not even the usual soda cans and snack bags. She walks barefoot on the wet sand, letting gentle waves lap over her skin, round the bluff to the spot where her mother liked to spread a blanket for picnics and stories.

She sits where her mother sat, looking at the full moon across the water. The light falling on the waves gives the impression of steps. She remembers the stories Rosalind told her on that blanket. On the night of a full moon, if you came to this exact spot, under the bluff, and stepped very carefully, you could walk the path of moonlight over the ocean and into another world. Mom said she had done this many times. As a child she played with secret friends and shared smoothies and ice-cream sundaes in a garden on the dark side of the moon. Later she went to a music school on the bright side of the moon, where she learned songs she sang at Tanglewood. Rosalind once confided that she had a very special teacher up there. When Diana asked his name, her mother would only call him the Man in the Moon.

Diana never tired of hearing these stories when she was small. When her body began to change, her attitude changed as well. She started to suspect that her mother was making everything up and had never been to the moon at all. By the time Diana reached middle school, she dismissed her mother's stories, along with fairy tales, as moonshine. But tonight she remembers what Rosalind whispered to her on that last day, when she was too weak to raise her head from the pillow. *Look for me by the path of moonlight on water.*

I miss you, Mom. Tears come now. She says it again, to the sea and the sand and the moon. I miss you so much. Without thinking, she is walking toward the water, to the exact place where the path of moonlight begins. There are footprints ahead of her on the sand. Startled, she stares around. The beach is still deserted, and there are no other footprints visible. Gingerly, she places a foot in one of the prints. It is a perfect fit. She tries again, with her other foot. Again the match is perfect. Did she walk to the water earlier? Grief must be muddling her memory.

She laughs at herself through the tears, as she places her left foot where the moonlight shines on the water. *I'm a silly little girl.* But she feels closer to her mother. The blade of grief that is swinging next to her heart loses some of its edge. She places her right foot on the path of moonlight. It's not solid, of course. How could it be? The sand is streaming under her feet. She pulls up her pant legs and steps further out. Her legs remain dry. And her feet. The surface beneath her undulates, but holds her up. This is of course impossible. But what did they say in that animated movie, the last film she saw with her mom? *It's only impossible if you think about it.*

What is the distance between the earth and the moon? It was a trick question in middle school. It depends on whether the moon is at its apogee or its perigee. There's a difference of thirty thousand miles. She can never remember which is which, and has no idea of what point in its orbit the moon might be in now. She is looking at the face in front of her. It is very definitely a face tonight, not a bunny. She has the crazy impression that an eye in the face is winking at her.

The path no longer holds her. She is falling. But she is falling *up*. She shudders, because the air is full of huge things with whirring limbs. They look like giant armored beetles. Her clothes are gone. They are mauling her, scrubbing and scraping. Dust particles are flying away. Now she is enveloped by something soft and feathery, like immense wings. She is being clothed again, in a simple white garment of the finest weave.

There is a door in front of her, floating in the sky. It opens, and she is in a garden bright with flowers, with wisteria and camellias, with hyacinths and wild roses. She walks a winding path over a little arched footbridge and looks down at fish sliding and glinting in a stream. On the far side of the bridge, a woman in a broad-brimmed straw hat garnished with a silk ribbon is pruning with a pair of shears.

The hat and the trailing ribbon are familiar. Diana remembers Rosalind's love of gardening, the hours she spent with photos of the gardens of Kyoto.

"Mom?"

The gardener turns, and Diana sees her mistake. This woman is younger than she is, no more than thirty, and in rosy good health. The next instant there is no distance between them. Diana is wrapped in an embrace. Her mother smells as she did when Rosalind came into her childhood room to tell bedtime stories and kiss her good night.

"It's really you! But how did you get to be so young?"

"Oh, sweetie, it's not so hard once you learn the way things work around here. We can look however we want to look. We don't have to dodder about like old sticks."

"You came to me in dreams, didn't you?"

"I tried to. Your door wasn't always open, and sometimes you were so sad that trying to reach you was like walking underwater."

"You always looked the way you did just before you left. Well, maybe the way you looked on a good day that year."

"I came to you in a way you would recognize. You weren't ready to see me a different way, so I had to put on the wrinkles and stoop, the way you put on makeup."

"Oh, Mommy, I've missed you so much."

Rosalind held her very close. "I never stopped thinking about you. And I have always been here for you."

They sat on a bench, and Diana's mother said, "You must give me an update on everything. Are you still with Joel?"

"Yes."

"And are things all right between you? Is he behaving himself?"

"We're still friends. You taught me that's the most important thing in a marriage."

"But you're not happy."

"I think it would be different if we'd been able to have a baby. But you know what happened."

Rosalind frowns and says, "That story may not be over."

"Mom? What do you mean? Do you know something?"

"Not yet, sweetie." Rosalind squeezes her hand. "But when I do know something, I'll let you know."

Diana cannot hold back the tears, of hope and of frustration. "You really can't say any more?"

"We learn here that life runs on many tracks. But I'm just a beginner. I can't see all of the patterns. All I can promise is that I'll be with you — and *for* you — in every way that I can."

Diana does not push the subject further. The pain of losing a baby early in her marriage to Joel is contending with the joy of being reunited with her mother. She never managed to get pregnant again, and the doctors told her that she must give up the dream of being a mother. She looks across the gardens to a pretty white cottage with a green door.

"Is all this real?"

"I've been working on it for a while," Rosalind smiles. "Would you believe that I've created a new rose and *three* new orchids? Come and look!"

The flowers are pretty but nothing extraordinary, in Diana's eyes. "I forgot." Rosalind pretends to slap herself on the side of the head. "You're not seeing beyond the spectrum you can see with your old-fashioned eyes. But there are still so many things I can show you. Where to begin? I know, we'll start with the Moon Café."

Diana follows her mother through an arbor of rambling roses to a gate in the garden wall. It opens into a scene that is so brilliantly white and busy that for a moment Diana has to shield her eyes. It could be Manhattan or Tokyo at theater time. High-rise buildings on all sides, people whirring between them through the air as well as on the ground.

Rosalind takes her daughter's hand, and they float effortlessly up to a roof terrace filled with people who are taking tea or sipping champagne within the folds of what seems to be a vast and elegant marquee.

"Do have a Bellini," Diana's mother insists. "It's nonalcoholic here, but it will still give you a lovely buzz." She signals for a waiter to bring the dessert cart. "And you must try the chocolate cake. You can eat whatever you like here and never put on weight."

Diana is amazed by the constant stream of people who pause at their table, kissing and hugging Rosalind like an intimate friend. Her mother was so reclusive in her last years.

A tall, dapper man with little wings of silver in his dark brown hair kisses Rosalind's hand and waits to be introduced.

"This is my friend Ronnie. He is an architect."

"You are as beautiful as your mother," Ronnie tells Diana, kissing her cheek. "Now I must ask to borrow her for a little while."

The band — unnoticed by Diana until now — is playing dance music. Diana's amazement deepens when she sees her mother whirled into a lively dance. Is she doing the foxtrot? A question dawns in her mind that makes her a little queasy.

When Rosalind returns to the table alone, flushed and happy, Diana puts the question directly. "How is Dad?"

Rosalind meets her eyes, hiding nothing. "I haven't seen him for some time. I've forgiven him for everything, if you are worried about that. But Henry has things to sort out in his own way, on a different level. And you know, people are not forced to stay together when we get here just because they were together somewhere else."

"Is Ronnie your — boyfriend?"

"He's a very good friend, and he makes me laugh. I think I deserve a bit of a vacation, don't you?"

Diana does not want to think about her mother having sex — what daughter does? — but the idea is in her mind. What would it be like to have sex on the moon? Like the Bellini, without some earthly ingredients, but wonderful?

Diana saw many things on that visit, with her mother as local guide. She saw the music school where Rosalind had received lessons, and met the opera singer who had showed her how to strengthen her voice. Diana giggled when the diva patted her midriff and told her, "Breathe from the diaphragm, dear. That's the trick."

They went down to a kind of landing, where new arrivals were being received and processed by welcoming committees. Some of the newcomers looked in vain for familiar faces. Their anxieties disappeared when kindly guides changed their looks to impersonate a departed loved one or a reassuring religious figure. It seemed that there was a kind of costume department for spiritual guides.

Diana clapped her hands when they went to the dog park. Happy dogs of every breed and combination were playing and running around, off leash. Then a big, sloppy black retriever was jumping on Diana, trying to lick her face. "Oh my God," Diana gasped. "It's Lulu." Tears of joy came now. She had loved Lulu so much as a child. She found a stick and threw it as far as she could. Lulu bounded after it and brought it back right away. She threw again and again, and Lulu was tireless, panting for more.

"She hasn't changed," Diana said to her mother. "She'll chase the stick for longer than my arm can hold up."

She looked more carefully around the dog park, noticing people who were approaching the field looking lost or sad or shy.

"This is a special place, isn't it?"

"Oh yes, sweetie. Dogs are the very best welcoming committee, because they love you no matter what. This is the best place for newcomers who are sad and shy to start their orientation."

There was a certain amount of form filling and identity checking going on at the landing. And now a huge vessel, like a multistory cruise ship, was docking and releasing droves of new arrivals.

"I didn't go through those controls," Diana observed.

"You are an invited guest, darling. Some of us are allowed to bring a visitor. And you did not escape the Scrubbers, did you?"

Despite her status as a guest, it was soon clear to Diana that much of this territory was off bounds.

When she wanted to go down a street leading off one of the great squares of the lunar city, her mother jerked her away forcefully, out of the way of a squad of policemen that rushed by. The policemen carried strange weapons shaped like giant leaves. They wore half-armor and had the heads of canines.

"There are bad neighborhoods in any world," Rosalind said.

They returned to the cottage. Rosalind was eager to show Diana how she arranged things. She had always had a flair for interior decoration. "I'm bored with this upholstery," she declared, over tea in her living room. She moved her hands as if stitching and the fabric changed, from floral to paisley. "Actually, I'm bored with the whole color scheme." She made a sweeping brushstroke in midair, and the walls were no longer blue but a warm orange spice.

Diana was drawn to a framed photograph of a sweet young girl. "Is this how you remember me, Mom? I don't remember seeing it before. Where was it taken?"

"Look closer, sweetie."

Diana picked up the photo. In her hands it became a window. She was looking into a happy scene with vibrant colors, ice-cream stands, beach umbrellas. In the midst of all this, the sweet young girl was waving to her.

For a moment, Diana's breath stopped.

"It's not — it can't be."

"But it can, sweetie. She couldn't come to you before, but she's been waiting."

"You mean — but the doctors said — "

"I can't promise you anything. But you two should get to know each other. She'll come to you in your dreams, and you'll come back to us here, and you'll figure things out together."

At that moment Diana remembered that though she was with her mother in that cottage of changing colors in the most tangible, palpable way, she must have a body somewhere else. She wasn't quite sure whether she had left it on the beach, or in bed before she went to the beach. With this thought came a stretching sensation, not unpleasant, like a really good, long stretch when she allowed herself a little extra time in bed on a rainy morning. As she continued to stretch, the scene around her began to blur into pointillist drips and splotches. Her mother waved through the dancing spots. "You'll come again! We'll be waiting for you!"

Conversation with a Daimon of Luna

Plutarch wrote that souls come and go constantly through the astral realm of Luna before birth and after death. He was not only a great historian and philosopher but a Mystery initiate, a priest of Apollo at Delphi, and a frequent visitor to the imaginal realm. In short, he probably knew what he was talking about. Plutarch maintained that the moon is the home of daimons — not to be confused with "demons" — including somewhat evolved spirits of the dead who take a close interest in human affairs and are very active in our dreams. Plutarch is great, and still held in great respect by scholars who have taken up residence in this realm. However, a daimon of Luna would like to bring us up to date.

Do you believe in the Man in the Moon?

No, not the face people imagine in the shadows of the craters, which is really the Great Rabbit, or Lunar Hare. Nor do I refer to those artful pictures, ever popular on greeting cards and in children's stories, that add a nose and a grin and a wink to the crescent moon.

I am speaking of something altogether different. I am inquiring whether you know anything (for worthwhile beliefs can only stem from knowledge) of the beings who live in the moon. I am well aware that since humans in clumsy space suits first walked on the moon, it has been commonly believed to be an astral desert, empty of organic life. This is merely a modern superstition, founded in the confusion of different orders of reality. Beyond appearances, the moon is thickly settled. Its inhabitants do not live *on* the moon in the way you live on the earth. They cannot be found on the lunar surface, from which astronauts and robots pick rock samples. The lunar population lives *in* the moon, which is to say, in the Sphere of Luna, a frequency domain located a little — *just* a little — beyond the realm you can touch and smell and taste with your ordinary senses.

I know what I am talking about, because the moon is my home. If you happen to meet me tonight, because you happen to be looking up at the bright face of the moon from under just the right tree at just the right time, or because you travel to my world on the wings of a dream, it's quite likely you might see me as the Man in the Moon, or at any rate *a* man in the moon. I find it generally convenient, in my dealings with humans, to show myself as a human male, taller than average, with what I conceive to be a commanding — though not overbearing — presence, exquisitely tailored in a mode that is rarely encountered on Earth outside Jermyn Street and one or two most particular establishments in Buenos Aires. Yet I must disclose, at the beginning of my tale, that "Man in the Moon" is a misnomer.

I live in the moon, but I am not a man. I am a daimon. I have lived very close to men, so close that I have sometimes forgotten my true identity. But I belong to a different and more ancient order of beings. When you turn to books, you will find the word *daimon* has several spellings. I prefer the oldest version, an accurate transliteration from the Greek, because the Greeks were close observers of traffic to and from my realm. Their witches — especially in the wild northern reaches — were adept at the dangerous art of drawing down spirits from the moon. The most excellent shaman-philosopher Plutarch studied deep in our academies before he took up permanent residence and joined the faculty of one of our finest schools. Plutarch's essay on the Sphere of Luna, *De facie quae in orbe lunae apparet*, remains the best travel guide to our realm outside the closed stacks of the Magic Library.

We know Plutarch well. It is a pity for you that his works are no longer taught in your schools, though he was read too often for what he wrote about tyrants and kings instead of for his essential work, which was all about us. He understood that the moon and the earth are as close as a man and his shadow. He knew that souls come and go constantly through our realm. He observed the descent of mind into the astral body in our dressing rooms, and the return of these energy suits to the suppliers when a traveler was given permission to return to the realm of mind. He watched all the souls that try to ascend to Luna after death and are rebuffed because they are dirty or confused. He saw souls that made it here, but who had reneged on their commitments, hurled from our ramparts through the black hole of Hecate. Do you know that great goddess's scary sister, Melinoe? No? Well, be thankful if she does not visit you in the night with her train of spooks and nightmares.

Do please be careful with the word *daimon* now that it is in the air, darting around you on dragonfly wings. Words have the power to call things into manifestation and bring creatures from one world into another. You don't want to say daimon out loud the wrong way; this can produce unpleasant effects, and sometimes unwanted visitors. I prefer to hear it pronounced *die-mon*, so it almost sounds like *diamond*, an elegant homonym. *Day-mon* is an acceptable alternative version. To call me a demon, on the other hand, would be extremely rude, as thoughtless as calling a man whose chosen name is Robert "Bob," and likely to produce more adverse effects than a frown and a growl. I did not mind being called a demon in demotic Greek in the age of Cleopatra, but since then a fog of fear and confusion spread by the morbid imaginations of the Dark Ages has made that version quite unusable.

Humans ask, across the soiled and bloodied centuries of their struggles, "Where was God?" The answer is quite simple, but impossible for devotees of a Solo Deity with a personal face to acknowledge. The One is everywhere, in everything, but does not intervene in human affairs. The Many *do* intervene, or interfere, quite frequently. They are a mixed bag. They bring both healing and harm. Some operate quite selflessly, out of compassion. Some have specific agendas, and require corresponding payoffs, care, and feeding. Some are agents of their orders, or of the interests of rival planetary intelligences competing for influence on the earth plane.

Cicero, that mellifluous skeptic, was correct (in the main) when he wrote that there are three things for humans to know about the gods: They exist. They take a close interest in mortal affairs. And they cannot be bribed.

The bribable entities are a gross and vulgar band, much sought after by the filthiest type of sorcerers.

I cannot be bribed, of course, but I am capable of being seduced. You should know that daimons fall in love, even as humans do.

We have a low boredom threshold. Our active help is engaged by those who live passionately and creatively, who burn with bright fire and move through life as shooting stars. We are called to those who take on impossible tasks, who leap over the abyss trusting that the bridge will appear or the wings unfold. Those we love make poetry of life. They tango with the emperor penguins, in the Antarctic gales, to keep the eggs warm while new life breaks through. They are travelers who always go beyond the road maps.

Maps are made of their journeys, and they use them to light fires in dark love nests, because they are already taking to the road from the place where their last journey ended.

I am willing to entertain questions, but be careful what you ask for.

How did I get here?

I can hear the words rattling round in your mind. You haven't been asking that question nearly enough. You open your door in a city and find yourself on top of a mountain, sometimes in your car, sometimes in a different body. You are watching a film, and you step through the screen and become one of the actors engaged in the drama. You think of a distant place, and the next moment you are there.

You have been here many times before, between many lives, but humans are forgetful animals. Part of you woke up from your walking sleep *down there*. But you would not have found me had I not found you first.

I have a question for you. Where is your body now?

I see this makes you a little dizzy. You see chasms opening below you, yes? But really it's not such a long drop. Take a look, but don't drop out of this conversation yet. There are many things you need to see and remember.

You call yourself a daimon. What about angels?

I am very glad to see so many humans writing and talking of angels. In this way, they acknowledge the existence of my kind, even if they often mistake our nature and functions.

If you must make distinctions, you could say that my kind have generally come up, while angels have generally come down. It is not a matter of dark or light, or of good and evil. There are dark angels, and there are very bright daimons.

I have heard that spirits transit this realm on the way to physical birth. Are there conditions for taking on a human body? Is a contract made before a soul goes down?

You don't get born into a human body without formalities. Everyone who is born on Earth has entered into a contract. A typical contract specifies the allotment of time-energy available to you in the life form you are entering. Time-energy is a package, not two different things. In the Assyrian language, we have a precise term: *shimtu*. The exact length of the life you are given may vary according to how carefully, or recklessly, you expend this time-energy. Living in balance, averaging a gentle cruising speed, you may manage a hundred years; treat your body like a hot rod and you can go to the junkyard early.

The life contract does not give ironclad protection against the events insurance companies call "acts of God," or against criminal interference.

You may end your life prematurely. This is a serious contractual violation that has unhappy consequences, though not the eternal damnation invented by some churchmen. Suicide is never part of a life contract. However, facing conditions that may tempt you to destroy yourself is quite often an important clause.

The allotment of time-energy is one of the two key elements in the contract. The other is the definition of the life assignment you have agreed to undertake.

Contrary to appearances, everyone born into a human body has agreed to their situation, though not everyone has the same degree of choice, and the choices that are made are often ill-considered.

One of the greatest acts of memory is to recall the terms of your life contract and who you were and where you were when you entered into it.

Who lives on Luna?

Permanent residents in my realm are few, though some of us live here for millennia by human counting.

We receive dreamers and soul travelers in vast numbers.

We are a transit lounge for spirits on their way to incarnation on Earth, and 'for ex-physicals who come up from the sublunar planes. Some of those admitted to this realm after death on Earth find solace for ages in our pleasure palaces and studios before they are ready for another death and another birth. Some pursue their studies in our schools, where many things are created and discovered before they manifest on Earth. Some become interpreters and teachers for physicals.

What is the work of these teachers?

It centers on the Art of Memory. Among humans, the most effective way to practice this is through dream recall and dream reentry. The memory of a dream is the memory of a journey. It may have been a short visit to a neighbor's house or the place you will find yourself on Tuesday next week. It may have been a far journey, to a distant galaxy or a vast dimension enfolded inside a pearl a hundred million billion times smaller than human instruments can detect in earth reality. Perhaps you were drawn *here*, to the Sphere of Luna, to study or to play in this realm.

So often the dream fades, or you abandon it, not trusting your memory. But when you hold to the dream, or let it gently return, a road opens before you. Move toward the dream space, and you travel between the worlds. Step fully inside the dream, and you are home, in its world.

Do you have a special language?

Only the most ancient among us still communicate in the language that Tehuti took to the land of Kem after he withdrew his light from the doomed temple of Atlantis. But we continue to use glyphs the lector-priests of Kem would recognize for our records.

As an interpreter, I am required to be fluent in all human thought-forms.

I have heard it said that Earth is now a cloaked planet, that the darkness around it makes it difficult for higher intelligences to get through to humans.

We are close to Earth here, as close as your dreams. But, as in your world, there are contending forces. Since the channels to Sirius have been disrupted, the Sirian ambassador often calls on me to translate messages for beings on the earth plane, and to arrange safe delivery. This of course means that I am now haunted by Ileaxu spies. We are a cockpit of intrigue, and every galactic power tries to push us from our neutrality.

It seems the Sirian connection is very important.

It holds the secret of the origin and purpose of the experiment with consciousness on Earth.

Who are the Ileaxu?

Forces inimical to human life. They seed chaos. You see their effects in places of power in your world. Be watchful. You may not know them yet, but they know you.

Are there Sirian envoys at work on Earth?

I will say nothing on this. But I can show you a memo prepared by another agency:

DETECTING A SIRIAN EMISSARY ON TERRA

1. Their auras are light blue, rising to a point 15–20 cm above the head.
2. They have a concealed "third eye," resembling a blue crystal, above and between the physical eyes.
3. They love water and can stay underwater longer than normal humans.
4. Dolphins recognize them and approach them spontaneously.
5. Dogs are drawn to them, and they are often found in the company of black dogs.

What can you tell me about parallel lives?

For the most part, humans inhabit time as a Lineland, a one-dimensional realm in which movement is possible only in relentless forward motion. Some humans are obscurely aware that in this forward motion they come to forks at which parallel times — and parallel worlds — split off. Only the rarest among them have been able to grasp that they are engaged with time like children in an elaborate jungle gym, with ladders and crosswalks that can take you to a different structure, swinging ropes that can fold distance, and chutes and ladders that can rocket you back to a point before the one where you started.

This is of course a preposterous simplification, since the maze is multidimensional, a Calabi-Yau environment rather than a jungle gym, and within it you encounter — and may be drawn into — other people's looping timelines.

Yes, you are living now in one of many parallel worlds. In some of those parallel realities, you have been living here with us, as a permanent resident, for many years.

You mean there are parallel worlds where I am already dead?

Why else is all of this so familiar to you? Why else would I talk to you? You understand, better than those who imagine that they are confined to a physical body, that your dreams are often glimpses of continuous lives you are living somewhere else.

How long do spirits remain in the realm of Luna after physical death?

Let's be clear that this is a gated community. You don't get in without paying your dues. There are many who are rejected at the gate, and some we have to throw out. They fall back into the astral slums below us that the Greeks called Hades.

Some discarnates spend the equivalent of many, many lifetimes here. They enjoy the social environment, they study and teach in our schools, they practice reality creation. Some become mentors and oracles for people on Earth. Some serve as messengers, zephyrs who carry dreams to sleepers.

If you earn the right to go higher, and choose to do that, you are given a new outfit, and you are required to leave your current vehicle behind. When you take off your astral body, you don't want to leave it lying around for anyone else to pick up. Depending on the quality, that could be like leaving a fur coat on the street. Someone is going to pick it up. Even if your threads are worn, they might be attractive to a passing spirit that wants to put on a new guise, or impersonate you, as a prank or for deliberate deception.

We have locker rooms where you can check your astral body as you would check your street clothes on the way to the gym.

Few of the graduates who leave astral bodies in these lockers will wish to retrieve them. Now equipped with celestial bodies — which don't fit over or under an astral suit — they know the joy of liberation from lesser forms and the appetites and cravings that go with them.

However, there are other uses for left-behind astral bodies. In the Messenger Service, some couriers are licensed to use these outfits in their encounters with people down below. So the deceased lover or father who visits a survivor could be that person, dropping by in the astral body — or an actor who has dressed up in that guise.

The actors or guisers should not be confused with the deceivers and thieves who hijack astral bodies for malign purposes. Their operations have sown much confusion and darkness.

Is reincarnation for real?

There is reincarnation, and then there is body-hopping. Don't get them mixed up. Reincarnation is what happens when a soul chooses to be born again in a different body after going through a process of cleanup, life review, and atonement. It takes time, although time works quite differently on the Other Side. It can't be rushed. A soul on the road of rebirth must rise to the understanding that there is karma from the previous life to be worked off, and that its new life situation is connected to what is going on with other members of its soul group. Before the descent into the amniotic lake, the reincarnating soul will be allowed to preview available life options. It will be given a glimpse of the place where it will be born, the parents who will provide the physical vehicle, and some (not all) of the episodes it will live on this possible event track.

We are not talking — yet — about the criminal souls. They will try to avoid entering the *bardo* realms for fear of having to face the consequences of their actions. They will rush through the first door that opens into any shady environment on the lower astral plane to hang out with their kind and repeat the things they enjoyed in life.

Let us move on to what the Greeks called *metempsychosis*. I prefer the muscular English expression *body-hopping*. You know this takes place in dreams. You find yourself in the body of a different person, perhaps a person of a different race or gender or social group. Remember your dreams of being in the body of the black basketball player (who was also a sexual athlete) and then the Dan Quayle body out on a golf course? Body-hopping dreams like these expand your humanity. You feel what it is like to live in someone else's skin. They also closely resemble the life-review options that are provided for those who have passed beyond the Plane of Recollection and are in the process of choosing a new life.

Now listen closely. When a soul avoids the bardo states and transfers directly from one body to another, its motives and condition may be splendid — even salvific — or very evil, or mixed.

Can I trust you?

I don't know everything. Omniscience is another department. I can assess probabilities. I can see across time and space, but even mortals can do that when they move beyond the superstition that their minds are locked up in their bodies and brains.

I am not infallible. There: I've said it. I hasten to add that even the Sirian ambassador makes mistakes. We are very far from perfection in the Sphere of Luna.

I would like to know your name.

I don't care what you call me, any more than your cat does. If *the Man in the Moon* seems too generic, or too much like something from the nursery, you can call me Polycrates. Look it up later if you must. We are constantly disappointed that you have forgotten your Greek. You swam in that language once like an olive in a jar of oil. I lived in many bodies in your world, and in a sense I still do, since I am required to check in with a number of people who are now my cases rather than my avatars. I am not your Higher Self, nor your genius. I am what I am: a daimon of Luna. I do send dreams to you, like moonbeams shining through your window. Sometimes, when you feel their touch, they become tractor beams, pulling you up into my realm.

You would not have found me if I had not been looking for you. You are here to remember, but you are going to see things you have not seen before, in any life, because we are changing faster than you could imagine. Constancy is not our forte in the realm of Luna.

Look at your earth from here. So very near, and so beautiful. But wait a moment.

I look, from your perspective. I see great ragged clouds, ranging in color from black to sickly quince, rolling across the earth. There are forms within them, ceaselessly swirling, like giant tumbleweeds, each composed of faces contorted with rage and pain. Cruel, misshapen beings move among them, goading.

This is why we call your world the Cloaked Planet. Your minds are occluded by the rushing thought-forms of those who were possessed by raging emotions and now seek to possess others. They are joined by entities that feed on violence. Some of these have never had human histories. Some are inimical to humans.

Early humans, who lived closer to the time when the Link

was formed, had a clearer understanding of where in the worlds you are. You live in an animate universe that is thickly populated with other forms of life and consciousness. These are generally invisible to you when you are in the physical body. What is it the Maya say? That when the gods succeeded in making men that could walk and talk and say thank-you to their makers, they became very worried when they saw that they had unintentionally given humans something approaching omniscience — that the two-leggeds they had made could see to and through all of Earth-Sky. So the gods decided to cloud the vision of humans. The gods breathed on the mirror of human minds. Picture acid rain coming down, or a good old Beijing smog. So humans go around in the equivalent of a London pea-souper from the heyday of coal.

And this is why you call Earth the Cloaked Planet?

That's not the half of it. Look up at the stars. Tell me what you see.

I see the Big Dipper. Wow, I can see the belt of Orion too. I didn't know you could find them in the sky at the same time. And Cygnus the Swan, is that right? I'm not very good at identifying constellations.

The stars care even less what you call them than I do. Humans look up and project different shapes and names, according to their imaginations, and then their descendants go on repeating those names through lack of imagination. There is what calls you, yes?

You point to the blue star. I am overcome, for a moment, by that deep longing, compounded of memory and desire, that the Portuguese call *saudade*.

Yes, you feel it deeply. The yearning for home. This is known to any of your kind who are not completely anesthetized and have not descended to the level of brutes. But hold your emotion for a moment. *This* is what you need to see.

The daimon reaches his arm up into the air. He pushes out a forefinger, apparently pointing out some pattern among the stars. Then he pinches his forefinger and thumb together, as if gathering fabric. With a gentle but determined motion, he pulls. The whole starry sky ripples, and an opening appears, as when the edge of a curtain is pulled back, just a little, to get a glimpse of the street. Through the gap, I see another dark sky, glinting with other stars. The daimon releases his grip, and the curtain is closed. I tell him:

You are a great illusionist. For a moment I thought you could actually roll up the night sky.

That is the illusion.

He gestures at the veil of the starry sky.

Which Is the Dream?

*I do not know how to distinguish between
waking life and a dream. Are we not always living
the life that we imagine we are?*

— HENRY DAVID THOREAU

1

I am leading a class in an arts center where I sometimes teach. A young woman asks, "How do I know I'm not dreaming now?"

"I'm not sure there is any way to establish that. But it is possible to know whether or not you are in a physical body."

To dramatize my point, I take a matchbook out of my pocket, strike a match, and hold the flame to the palm of my hand. I feel heat and then a little pain. "Or like this." I move the flame to the unlit candle on a low table at the center of the room. When the wick is lit, I wait for hot liquid wax to pool around it. Then I cup my hand and dribble the hot wax onto it. This hurts a lot.

I restore the candle to the table, wipe my hand, and say, "I guess I just proved that I am not dreaming in the sense that I am in my physical body."

This produces chuckles, then laughter that seems louder and deeper than our little group could produce. The laughter is rocking the room. Paintings are sliding off their hooks. The tall windows overlooking the gardens fly open with a bang.

The crash blurs my senses. Now I am in bed. I look at my hand. There is a rose-colored bruise in the center of my palm. Was I dreaming when I burned myself with the candle wax, or am I dreaming now?

I go to my office to add to my file on Reality Tests. I am pleased to see the dossier is growing thick and rich. Someone is tapping at the French doors to my study. It's my neighbor. I pop a can of beer for him — he's always ready — and start telling him, "I've got fantastic stuff here."

"What's it about?"

"It's about reality."

"I read this sci-fi story. It says that reality is what goes on happening even after you stop believing in it."

"That's pretty good." I make a note of it.

Then I notice I am writing with my left hand. I don't do that.

"Jimmy, I don't know which is the dream!"

"I'll drink to that."

I was back in bed. I stretched, showered, and walked the dog. He was soon checking the news with his nose. I pulled a dead maple leaf off his snout. The park was clearly real to him, and to his snout.

I counted my false awakenings so far that day. I wasn't satisfied that I completed the list, even as I cleaned up after the dog with a plastic bag, which has to be one of the least dreamy things you can do.

My reality test with the candle wax was obviously a dud. Or was it? Maybe it had shown me something more interesting than the bald distinction between waking and dreaming. The dream body knows pleasure and pain. It has senses, just like the physical body. What happens to it can even leave a mark on the regular body. I turned over my hand. The palm was still lipstick pink.

A dream world is real. It has its own physics. For someone living in a dream world, or even just passing through, it is the regular world that seems hazy, fleeting, or hallucinated.

2

There I go again. I am with someone who was very close to me many years ago. We are holding a dinner party together, and I am proud of the elegant dining set I have purchased. The table can seat twenty people quite comfortably, and cheerful guests are taking their seats.

I want to tell the group how I came to buy this table. I ask if anyone knows the story.

Patricia Garfield, a famous dream author, raises her hand, turning from her place at the table.

I am going to tell my story anyway. It involves a visit to a "cheap" Sotheby's auction in London, not one of the grand auctions. My purchase of this table marked a turning point in my life. I now believe that without the table — and its promise of engagement with large, convivial groups in a social setting — my life would have taken a different course, and I would not have remained close to the woman who is responsible for tonight's party.

When I step outside the house for a moment, into bright sunlight, I realize that in the reality where my body is asleep in bed, the woman I am with is dead. She died many years ago.

So I am in a dream.

I look back at the house. It is a row house in London, like houses I lived in long ago. The scene is entirely real, and solid — the portly taxi pulling up near the steps, the couple with a baby in a perambulator, the sounds from the house.

Is the me that is in bed in upstate New York dreaming me, or am I dreaming him?

I am in a place where someone who died in one world is alive in another.

This feels less like an afterlife situation than like a parallel reality, an alternate world, where she is alive and I made radically different life choices.

I returned from this dream excursion feeling calm and reflective, saddened by memories of the loss of a wonderful woman who died tragically young, cheered by the idea that she may be enjoying a happy life in another reality, and maybe in many alternate realities.

It's a common, perhaps even universal experience to find that the dead are alive in our dreams.

Often an encounter with the dead in a dream becomes a prompt to dream lucidity. As we begin to realize that someone we are with has died (in our default reality), an inner voice may say, *I am dreaming.*

The presence of Patricia Garfield, the dream author, may have been a prompt to the Robert at that dinner table to say to himself, *I am dreaming.*

There are things of huge importance afoot.

Encounters with the dead, especially in dreams, have been a primary source of human knowledge of the afterlife throughout the whole odyssey of our kind on the planet. More than this, we may come to understand that in dreams and visions, we are at home in the realities where those who died in this world are at home. We don't need to puzzle over what happens in the afterlife once we realize that we are already in it.

As I write this, I am back in a world that I know is real through the evidence of my senses. My left instep hurts a bit, the legacy of excessive hill walking in recent travels. I hear the Bluetoothed mailman talking to unseen persons as he walks the street. I sense my fierce, bad kitten trying to sneak into my study to turn it into a toy room.

Yet my senses were no less alive when I was welcoming guests at the enormous dining table. I could smell the aromas of cooking from the kitchen and of the flower arrangements on the table. I could feel sun on my face when I stepped outside.

I muse over the many ways in which the Robert who is at home in that scene is different from my present self. He is highly social, very willing to entertain twenty or more people in his own home. By contrast, the Robert who is writing now is fiercely private at home and avoids social scenes, except in the context of his chosen work. (I often sit down to dinner with twenty people when I am leading residential retreats.)

Yes, the dinner scene where someone dead was alive is a dream. And it is entirely real. Like life. Here and there, now and then.

3

A knock on the door before dawn. I rise groggy from another country, my heart pounding from the wild action scene I have just been in. It takes me a moment to identify where I am, and a moment more to pull on a T-shirt and answer the door.

There's nobody there. I stick my head out and inspect the corridor, lit only by the dull orange glow of the night-lights. No one — except for a dim figure with hair sticking up like white hay in the wall mirror by the bathroom. I wasn't dressed like that in the place I've just returned from. My hair was neatly barbered and brushed.

I pad in my bare feet toward my mirror self. As I brush my teeth, I try to pull back the details of my latest expedition, the one from which the unexplained knock at the door has recalled me. I was in Moscow. I was privy to a crisis meeting of top executives from two Western corporations. They feared they were being chiseled out of their fair share of the earnings from a joint venture with Russians after taking most of the risk and laying out most of the cash. Not the kind of news I follow anymore, and not a scene to which anyone would invite my regular self.

Let's see. After that meeting, I went with a Russian companion to a private club where post-Soviet cowboy capitalists hang out. There was a group of pasty, self-important men in skimpy black swimsuits by a large indoor pool. As my companion led the way toward them, one of them grabbed for something under his recliner and came up with a gun, a stubby automatic weapon. My Russian friend moved at lightning speed, wrested the gun away from him, and used it against him. The gun must have been fitted with a silencer, because the shots were almost noiseless.

This rapid, ruthless action left the Moscow mafiosi shock-still. I don't know what happened next, because the mysterious knocking at my door pulled me back into my room more than a continent away, from Moscow to the foothills of the Cascades.

We dream in many ways, and it is important to notice that very different things may be going on in different types of dreaming. My Moscow action thriller might sound like a movie scene, but for my dream self — and my waking self, when first aroused — it was altogether *real*. When I ask, "Whose body am I in?" I have no doubt that it is my own body, though it has been used somewhat differently than the body in which I am typing this, and has the attentions of the kind of tailor I haven't frequented in decades. For an equally long period, I have led a peaceable life devoted to teaching, writing, healing, and building my dream school. I don't follow the news closely. I have no access to corporate bosses and no inclination to run around with secret agents or get anywhere near shoot-'em-ups. But my dream self seems to be leading a very different life.

Jung might call this *compensation*, meaning that what goes on in dreams may give us a taste of a life unlived in ordinary days. Thus the ascetic priest in a Théophile Gautier story spends his nights as a randy libertine. This explanation doesn't satisfy me. Nor does the scenario of the old *Quantum Leap* TV series, in which the hero is catapulted into different bodies to manage different crises — though I have dreams like this too. No, I think that I was recalled by the knock on the door from an adventure of one of my parallel selves, a self who made different choices from the man writing this line — a fellow (for example) who remained an international journalist able to open doors all over the world, ever-eager to predict the next moves in the great game of nations.

What would you be doing if you had stayed in that marriage you left, or the old job, or (alternatively) had taken that risk and gone off to Samoa instead of taking that postgrad degree? In dreams, you can find yourself in the thick of *the alternate lives you may be leading now,* among the possibly infinite parallel universes that leading-edge physicists tell us are a probability.

The unexplained knock on the door pulled me out of a parallel life adventure. It cut my experience short but may have gotten me out of trouble; I'm sure there was more gunplay ahead. Knocked out of the dream, I retained *something* — a vivid flash of memory that might have slipped away completely had I made a smoother return from that other country.

So perhaps I should give thanks to the unknown fist at my

door that pulled me back. But wait a minute. On which side of the door was the knocking?

4

It was snowing over the new Denver airport as I boarded the shuttle bus for my hotel. My suitcase was flying somewhere without me. I had left home at the start of a warm, bright end-of-summer day — warm enough to swim in the pool, which was still open — bound for Boise via Chicago. Storms in the Midwest, mechanical trouble, and missed connections had bumped me to Detroit and dumped me in Denver snow, well after midnight, en route to a ghost airport.

Planes no longer flew from the old Stapleton field, but the look-alike airport hotels clung like crabgrass to the perimeter of its *terrain vague.*

How do I know I'm not dreaming? I asked myself as I rode up in the glass cage of the hotel elevator. The seasons were scrambled; I had spent all day traveling to places that were not on my itinerary, and I had ended up at an airport from which planes do not take off. As a matter of fact, how did I know I wasn't dead? In dreams, I have noticed that luggage is sometimes a metaphor for the physical body, as well as for life burdens. Here I was, beside a ghost airport, without my bag. Could it be I had lost my bag of meat and bones?

I called my friend in Boise. There was static on the line, but he seemed to understand me well enough. This seemed to indicate that I was not dead or dreaming — until I remembered that in dreams, we quite frequently receive phone calls from the departed. What evidence did I have that I was not one of those dead people who phone the living in their dreams?

Only the minor discomforts of the flesh: a mildly upset stomach, the pricking of stubble I pecked at with the little pink throwaway razor they had given me at the hotel reception desk. I showered until my skin shone red as a boiled lobster. The depth and texture of all these corporeal sensations were proof, surely, that I was fully inside my physical body and was therefore neither dead nor dreaming.

Yet, I reflected, the play of the senses is not confined to the physical plane. The dream body has its own sensory array and experiences touch and smell and taste as well as sight and sound, as well as a finer range of perception mediated by finer antennae.

I resolved to dream on my problem. I tossed for a long time on an uncomfortable cusp of sleep, disturbed by the psychic litter you routinely encounter in places frequented by transients: the fantasies and nightmares of traveling salesmen, flight attendants, and (on this particular night) prison wardens, who had been in town for a conference. I watched the tawdry show for a couple of hours before I fell out of my body and into the sky.

> I am flying under a snowy sky, over an airfield from which planes never take off. Below me are anonymous rooftops. I can't tell one building from another. I'm having a hard time remembering where I left my body. It's in one of these hotels, but I can't for the life of me remember which one. Something tugs at me, and I decide to take a chance. I dive down through one of the rooftops and land with a huge whoomph in the body on the bed.

I opened my eyes, feeling bruised and disoriented. I recognized nothing in my environment, nothing that pertained to me. For a ghastly moment, not only did I not know where I was, I did not know *who* I was. I retained my sense of self. In a larger sense, I knew perfectly well who I was. But for a moment I had forgotten what identity and what body I had chosen to inhabit.

I recovered from my partial amnesia within seconds, but it was a shocker. It was still percolating as the morning shuttle carried me across the high plateau toward the nested cones of the new airport terminal.

The path of the soul after death, say the Plains Indians, is the path of the soul in dreams — except that you don't get to come back (however bumpily) to the same physical body. Given my confusion, coming and going from the dream state, is it any wonder that people get lost and confused after physical death?

5

In dreams, you may check in to a parallel life you are leading somewhere else.

You may be swimming with seals, or looking for the selkie skin that was hidden from you. You might still be living with your ex, doing the things you would be doing if you had never broken up. You might be marching with those warriors in leather armor under the banner of a bear goddess. You might be running that bordello in the French Quarter in old New Orleans. You may be up on a high rooftop, looking down on your present life in the perspective of the Double on the Balcony, your eternal witness.

When you exit a dream that is also a visit to a parallel life, your parallel self continues on its way. While you go about your day, your other self may dream of you.

Jung struggled for clarity on this issue, and found it late in life. He came to believe that we lead continuous lives in our dreams. Put another way, your dream may be a glimpse of a continuous life you are living somewhere else, a life that goes on whether or not you are tuned to its channel. This is something you can dream on.

You get up in the middle of the night and go to the bathroom. When you return to bed, you find the same dream is playing as you were dreaming before, but the action has moved along. A bathroom break may be the start of your awakening.

Sometimes a dream of this kind reaches to you from another realm like a giant fist, pulling you in and back. It was like that for me one night at Big Sur. I was in a bed overlooking the Pacific Ocean, my window open to catch the sea breeze and the marvelous rhythm of the waves breaking on the rocky shore.

In my dreams, I was far away, in Mongolia in a cruel winter, on the eve of World War II. I was engaged in a secret mission — to spy on a team of SS commandos who were seeking to capture the most powerful shamanic artifact in Central Asia: the spirit banner of Genghis Khan. I stirred from this dream, thrilled and mystified. I might have made it my plan to reenter the dream to try to understand why I was in Mongolia in the 1930s while my body was on the California coast. But no effort on my part was required — unless I had wanted to resist going back.

Again and again, through the whole night, the drama played on. All my senses were engaged. Now in a dual or multiple state of consciousness, I could hear the Pacific breakers and turn on the bed while being fully present in the Mongolian adventure in a body that felt no less real. I could taste the blood from a horse's neck I was required to drink in order to survive that terrible winter, in a wilderness of snow. I could smell the rank fear of horses and men. I have no doubt I was *there*.

6

Some dreamscapes appear to be stage sets. You step into the wings, and the scene is changed, or gone completely. Some are pocket realities; go outside and there is no *there* there.

When I become lucid, I sometimes explore the borders of these landscapes. Once I was deep in an adventure in a rainforest. When I became aware I was dreaming, I marched off in a certain direction — to find that I came to a line where the jungle, and its world, simply ended. When I traveled through the forest in other directions, I found the same thing. Beyond the jungle world, on every side, there was nothing but a white void. Its color and texture resembled the drawing paper on which I proceeded to sketch this geography.

Night after night, in a certain interval of terror and beauty in my life, I was carried away to a mountain convent that was a complete world, for training and initiation by an order of priestesses. How a mountain can be a planet, except in a painting by Magritte or a story by Saint-Exupéry, is a question no dreamer needs to ask. The shape of the world mountain, when I drew it, looked like a bobbing toy, the kind you could float in a bathtub. Around it was the vastness of space, not dark or drawing-paper white, but grainy and silvery like mother-of-pearl.

One night, I was deep in magical intrigues in a vast apartment in a huge old building in an old European city. With companions, I moved from room to room, accessed by wide, long halls that turned back upon themselves, counterclockwise, like Greek keys. Sometimes a hall would end, without explanation, at a blank wall or sealed door.

The following night, in my dream body, I walked cobbled streets, under arches, in another Old World city, perhaps Prague. I again had the sense that I was being directed, unobtrusively, to turn in a counterclockwise spiral. Before me walked a man who was looking at me from the back of his head. It was hard to tell whether the face on his back was a mask or a double. Behind me walked a second man with two faces. Their presence was deliciously creepy, but in no way sinister or threatening, during or after the dream. Though the city was dark and silent in the dream, there was a feeling of carnival, of dress-up.

7

In some of my favorite dreams — though I don't call them that until I leave them — I am already dead to this world. I am living a wonderful life, teaching and studying in a school of advanced studies on the Other Side. With my favorite dead professor, I study parallel lives in the School of Metahistory, observing how the dramas of a personality in one time turn on a life in another time like cogwheels. In the Department of Literary Production, I enjoy beaming ideas for books and scripts to writers who can manifest them and save me the labor of pecking at a keyboard. This is so much fun that it helps me understand why angels and creative daimons do what they do.

I enjoy my time in the Communications Center. There are so many people who are eager to contact a survivor but have trouble getting through. Sometimes, when the message they need to send is urgent, they are allowed to enlist the help of the Zephyr Corps. The zephyrs are the bravest among our couriers. You may know them by their winged feet, though they move so quickly and subtly that most people fail to see them at all. They can slip through the smallest aperture.

In this world I have a beautiful penthouse apartment with a huge terrace swimming pool. I can dive twenty stories down, from the edge of the terrace into the perfect blue water of a bay, where I swim underwater and then fly up into the air. Physics works differently here! When I first joined my parallel self over here, I was curious to see that I have a bed, since sleep is not necessary here, except as part of the weaning of old habits. Lovemaking is possible, though the experience is more like the full-body weaving of electrical energies (as depicted in *Cocoon*) than like physical sex. I lay down on the bed to see what dreaming is like here. Immediately I was contained in a holographic field where my dreams played out all around me, engaging all the senses. I have yet to determine whether these dreams are being produced or are selected from an existing library.

Dog Shows

Dogs love us no matter what. Maybe they love us enough
to send us dreams.

1

The Viennese love their dogs and take them everywhere. Last
night I stopped at a *beisl* — bistro — in the Inner City and saw
a dog eating from his own plate at a table where hard-faced men
in the jewelry trade were inspecting stones through their loupes.

So, on a flat gray morning with the sky lying over the city like
an iron lid, I am not altogether surprised to receive an invitation
to a dog show, pushed under the door of my hotel room. The invitation arrives in a fine envelope, my name perfectly formed in a
looping hand. It is signed with the print of a dog's paw. Very cute.

I have nothing planned for the afternoon, and the address is
an easy walk from the hotel, so I stroll that way after some work at
the library and coffee at the Café Central.

They take my coat at reception, and an attendant in formal

livery opens the door to the showroom. I am startled to find this is not the usual open space but a conference hall, with banked seats. The sight of the speaker stops my heart.

He is Kipling, my beloved black dog. This is impossible, because he was killed on the road many years ago, on a night before Halloween. Yet when he glances my way and cocks his ears, I am sure of it. I am so stunned by his appearance here that it does not strike me as odd that he is speaking, with eloquence and passion, in a language I can understand.

"Dogs have a vital role to play in helping their humans to survive," the big black dog declares. "The human animal needs not only food and water and air and love; he requires something called *meaning* or *purpose*. The best way to put humans in touch with purpose is to bring them back into contact with their dreams."

Some of the Viennese dogs object that they are already giving their humans the best thing. "We love them no matter what. We love them no matter how they treat us, and we are always there for them."

"It's not enough," Kipling says firmly, ears pricked.

A Viennese dog named Viktor speaks in support of my dog. "In Vienna, there is no doubt that man requires meaning. It was the lack of a personal sense of meaning that produced the collective nightmares that were born here and threaten to return.

"We dogs of Vienna," he insists, "must take on the role of soul guide at night."

Several voices are raised, demanding practical details.

"We will create a film company. We will produce movies that humans will see in their dreams."

The motion is carried overwhelmingly, with much tail-wagging.

Kipling comes down from the platform and says, "Let's go for a walk."

He has a leash in his mouth and encourages me to yoke it to his collar. We don't want to scare the humans.

We walk through the immense park that surrounds the baroque pile of the Schönbrunn palace, desolate and melancholy in this season. We encounter the old Emperor Franz Josef. He has stepped down from his plinth and is walking around a fountain. My black dog, with fine deliberation, lifts his leg and pees on the emperor's leg.

2

Jeb Panic isn't a bad man. His two German shepherds know that he loves them. He just doesn't understand them. He lives on a fine spread in Virginia, an hour's drive from the capital. But Jeb is getting on and doesn't get around so well anymore, even after the hip replacement. He can't walk the big dogs far, and it would be cruel to keep them cooped up in a kennel. So he lets them run free. He wants to make sure they come when they are called, so he has them fitted with electronic collars. He zaps them when he wants them back in the house.

I tell Jeb this is no way to treat dogs. He bristles. He insists his dogs don't mind. It's only a buzzer going off, like that thing they give you in family restaurants to let you know when your table is ready.

I guess Jeb does not know about the dogs' film company.

He comes into the kitchen white-faced the next morning.

When I ask him what's the matter, he mutters something about a dream. Jeb isn't much into telling dreams, so he has my immediate attention.

"Do you want to tell me the dream?"

"Oh, it's nothing. Some Nazi shit. Probably the result of what's going on in Washington."

"Try it on me."

He gulps his coffee, clears his throat, and starts like this: "I'm in a Nazi concentration camp. Those bastards are parading up and down with their guard dogs, which snarl at me if I step one inch out of line. I'm in a yard, fitted with an electronic collar. When they want me for something, they zap me, and I feel throttled."

He runs a hand around his throat, reliving the searing pain of the collar in shock mode.

"If it were my dream," I say to Jeb, "I might think that my dogs had produced this for me to let me know how they feel when I zap them on their electronic collars."

"Get outta here," says Jeb.

He means it literally. He makes it very clear he doesn't want me around after this. He isn't ready to hear from his dogs. When I say good-bye to them, I whisper, "Do it again, and again. Put him back in that scene until he gets it. Humans can be very slow. Sometimes they need a dream to repeat over and over before they get the message and are ready to do something about it."

When the Same Dream Keeps Playing

Are you fed up with the same dream coming again and again? Has it occurred to you that your dream-production crew, behind the scenes, may be even more fed up with having to make the same movie for you over and over because you don't get the message or won't act on it?

"Merde." It sounded less rude in French. But when the registrar told her, "There is no getting out of this," Monique said it in English and stamped her foot.

"Don't you understand that I graduated bloody *thirty years* ago?" she all but spat at him. "Do I have to go home and take my fucking degree certificate out of the frame?"

"None of that alters the situation," the registrar said quietly but firmly. He sighted along a metal ruler as if to reinforce the firmness of this ruling. Who even uses a ruler these days?

"I don't even have a schedule for the exams. I don't know the subjects, or what is required."

"Do some research. Ask around. Look it up. I am not a public information booth."

"Shit." Monique slammed the door as she left the office. This drew a backward look from a man walking along the hall.

"Excuse me," she chanced it. "Are you taking the med finals next week?"

"Why do you ask?" He is absolutely gorgeous, she thought. He would be almost too pretty in that powder-blue cashmere sweater and neck scarf wound the French way, except for those broad shoulders and — she checked — the promising bulge down below. She may have been vamping just a bit when she told him, "I'm taking the exams myself, and I'm looking for just a teensy bit of information."

"Really? Well, I suppose it's never too late to start."

It hit her that he was thirty years younger. He was the age she was when she took these exams that she was being told to take again. She really wished they had been in the same class back then. Now she was thirty effing years too old for him.

"So you are taking the exams next week."

"Starting Monday morning. Is there some way I can help you?" He sounded as if he was volunteering to assist an old lady to cross the street.

"I've lost track of the schedule." This was true enough. "I've forgotten what we're sitting for on Monday."

"Pharmacology."

Merde, shit, fuck. You had to remember so many details for that, all those mechanisms of actions, side effects, and interactions.

"And the prescribed texts are?"

He gave her the titles of two fat textbooks, frowning a little.

"You really are starting rather late," he said to her. He was right about that. These were not the texts she had worked with thirty years ago. "Have you even looked at the books?"

"Um, I don't actually have copies."

"Well, if you hop it, you might be able to get them from the bookshop. You do have the weekend, after all. But the shop closes in ten minutes, I believe."

"Thanks." She was running out the door. She tripped over a grate in her high heels and pulled them off.

"If all else fails," he called after her, "there's always gin!"

The bookshop was where it used to be, one block up and a turn to the left. But they were locking up. She tapped on the glass door and gave her most flirtatious smile.

"Sorry, luv, you'll have to come back in the morning."

Once again, she was thirty years too late.

She yelled on the street, more like someone with Tourette's — she wrote a paper on that, thirty years ago — than like a person on Bluetooth. "I did my exams. I've got my degree! Why the hell am I being made to go through this again!"

We are watching her from up in the gods. The cast withdraw from the film set. Through the curtain we see her groaning as "Flight of the Bumblebee," from the smartphone she parks on her bedside table, pulls her out of the entertainment we have produced for her.

"She's becoming aware," says one of the producers. "This time she remembered that she took the exams thirty years ago. She missed that fact in the first thirty-two — no, thirty-three — cuts."

"And now she's remembering a bit more from her dreams," says one of the sound crew. "She's asking why she keeps having the same dream."

"I don't want to rain on your parade," the handsome young actor calls up to us. He's still in that powder-blue pullover, with a lock falling ever so charmingly over his aristocratic brow. "But we are all getting *bloody* fed up with this production. Do you know how boring it is to have to recite the same lines about textbooks over and over again?"

"He always wants to be a romantic lead," sniffs the actor who played registrar.

The guild representative clears his throat. An officious little twerp, but we have to hear him out. "You people up there should know that half the crew are ready to stage a walkout. How many repeats of these formula flicks are we supposed to make for this woman? Have you been listening in to her since she woke up? She's moaning to a friend that she is stuck in Exam Land and doesn't know why. *We* are all stuck in Exam Land with her until she gets the message and does something about it."

We appraise the situation over a light lunch. Monique, we agree, has made some progress. In the latest session, she remembered, as the scene repeated yet again, that she passed her exams and got her degree years ago. However, she remains clueless about how the recurring theme of taking a test may apply to what is going on and coming up in her life now. We know exactly what is coming up for her. That's why we developed the script we are using for the dream we are producing. She's thinking about a new job in her medical field that will require her to bone up on a lot of texts and new material very fast. She may be dimly aware that all of human life is a school, with many tests and classes you have to take over until you make your grades.

What she doesn't grasp yet is that she needs to write her own script. She'll soon be required to do that in any event, since our best scriptwriters are tired of reissuing the same boring screenplay with just minor tweaks. The actor who is just a supporting player in the current version of her movie wants to be the romantic lead in a better drama.

She doesn't get it yet, we agree.

So we'll have to run the same damn film over and over. That is, if the production crew doesn't go on strike. We have been told, up here among the gods, that strike action is brewing. Our kind don't have infinite patience with humans.

Do You Still Fool Around?

When do you start to suspect that you are dreaming? When the black cat walks across the room in the same direction twice? When you look in a mirror and see a different face? When you realize that the people you are partying with are all dead in the ordinary world?

How long would it take for you to become lucid if you found yourself about to have sex in front of cameras with a movie-star-handsome guy? Would you then leave the dream, or stay in it? Let's listen to Greta's story.

"Do you still fool around?" Betty asks.

When she tells me what she has in mind, I say, "Get outta here." She's a couple of mai tais ahead of me. We were party girls back in college, and stayed friends through several divorces and one partner exchange. But this isn't funny.

"They want *me*?"

"Like I said."

"And they want me to do what, exactly?"

"Come on, Greta, we may have put some mileage on the clock, but we haven't forgotten how the parts work."

"You're telling me they want me to have sex in front of a room full of people."

"It's for science, remember?"

I can feel the heat in my face. Betty has to be pulling my leg, yet I have the funny feeling this is for real. Betty persuaded me to sit in with an evening group that is supposed be studying the physiology of sexual responses, from foreplay to full-body orgasm. I told her this was just an excuse for old people to watch X-rated movies. In our case, female Viagra. Until now, the presentations have been as exciting as watching amoebas subdivide. I can't say how long the sessions have been going on. Screen images run through my mind, then stutter or fade or repeat in reverse order, like an old-time movie projector crapping out.

Now Betty is telling me the study is perking up. They are going to use live sex partners, wired up so every slosh and tremor can be recorded. And the committee has selected me to be the first female lab rat.

"So who's the lucky guy?" If this is for real, I know what's coming next. My partner is going to be Al, a snowbird who is too cheap to pay for tooth implants and tries to get his hand on my sensitive bits during the videos. He must be north of eighty.

Betty shakes her head. "He's a new guy. And he's gorgeous. Think Richard Gere, add six inches, and take away twenty years. I swear to God. I've seen his picture."

I slide between disbelief, embarrassment, and an oh-so-delicious hunger. "How come you have the inside track?"

"I'm on the committee, darling. You know I'd volunteer myself, but you have so much more pizzazz and sexiness than I do." She pouts when she adds, "And you're the one they want!"

"And this is supposed to happen when?"

"Bottoms up. We're starting right away."

I don't know how my drink vanished, or who paid for the tab, or how we got from the bar to the meeting room without walking or hailing a cab.

We are simply there, in the big basement set up like a fifties rec room with games and folding chairs. They have dragged a pool table into the middle of the space, under a horrible strip light. This is evidently where the game is to be played. They have set up chairs all around so people can watch from up close and take notes and pictures. There are many more people than usual, phone cameras at the ready.

I survey the pool table, and Al fingering his dentures, and the pudgy broker next to him wiping his smudged glasses so he won't miss any close-up action. I am ready to walk out when *he* comes in, holding Betty's hand. How did she manage to meet him at the door when she was next to me a moment ago?

The question dies unanswered, because he is everything she promised. A thirty-something Richard Gere who has grown a head higher. My nerve endings are waving like sea anemones in a feeding frenzy. We make eye contact, and I hear the sappy soundtrack that plays when two lovers meet in an old movie. My imagination is racing ahead in anticipation as he walks toward me with a smile and eyes focused only on me. As he gets closer, I see he is really taking me in from my legs to my hair with total admiration and appreciation. This is going to be amazing. He reaches for my hand, and I feel the warmth spread up my arm and rush all through my body.

"I'm too old for this," I say to no one in particular.

"You are in your prime," says Richard Gere. "A real man knows that a woman your age is at her peak. Men fear you because they can't keep up, or keep it up. You can have a hundred orgasms for one of mine, but that doesn't scare me at all, because you are the woman I've been waiting for."

I can't believe I am wet inside my panties.

The crowd erupts. It's as loud as a political rally.

The heat inside me is gushing from my breasts to my groin. My face must be as red as a juicy red apple. I can't look at the floor, because I may be dripping.

The crowd is bigger than before, vastly bigger.

Someone says they are moving us to a larger space.

We are there right away. It's a huge open-plan studio near the top of a high-rise building. I can't see the view outside, because people are packed in on all sides. They are on faux-leather swivel chairs. They are squatting on the floor. They are standing shoulder to shoulder in front of the windows.

Someone waves to me. I recognize my favorite professor from college. How come he's looking so good, like he hasn't aged at all?

They have substituted a king-size bed for the pool table. It must have come straight from the furniture store; I can see the tags. It's raised up on a kind of platform, and there are lights and cameras poking in from all sides.

I'm really scared now, but Richard Gere has his hand on the small of my back and is murmuring, "You'll be fine. You are beautiful."

It's for science, I remind myself.

I let him unbutton my blouse. When I reach for his belt buckle, I see he is more than ready. I pull down my skirt. I let him unhook my bra. I wait until I am between the sheets before I take off my panties.

I'm not thinking about the crowds or the cameras now. I'm thinking about what it will feel like to have him inside me. There's a long delay while people stick electrodes and sensors all over me. I wonder how Richard Gere will look with sensors or miniaturized cameras on his cock, and how we can do anything if he comes on to me that way.

I realize now that I haven't taken off my panties. This is crazy. I took them off already. Why are they still on? I pull them off and kick them to the bottom of the bed.

A woman comes to stick on more sensors. She is really excited about this and can't stop talking about how we are making a film that will be watched by millions. This is really scary, but I'm not listening closely, because I still have my panties on.

I start to pull them off for, what, the third time. This dumb repetition jolts something in my head. Things don't repeat like this normally, even with an idiot. There's something really off.

I close my eyes.

When I open them, I'm in my normal bed, and I'm not wearing panties. No Richard Gere, no lights and cameras, no audience of millions. Did I come away too soon, missing my big scene? Can I find my way there again? I close my eyes, wishing myself in the bed in the dream studio. All I see is a floater under my eyelid.

I reach for my phone and call Betty. Does she want to go someplace and drink mai tais tonight? Sure. She had the exact same idea. "In fact," she says, "I've got an interesting proposition for you."

Where Women Have Four Husbands

I am on my way with a woman companion to the Palais de Justice in Paris. An angry gendarme is waving at us to hurry up, hurry up, because our taxi is double-parked on a curving street. To keep up with my companion, who is running in her high heels, I take off my own shoes, which have very high heels and straps. I don't find it unusual that I am wearing a woman's shoes until I fall out of the dream without ever feeling that my visit to Paris is less than real.

I think about other dreams in which I have noticed myself wearing women's shoes. Sometimes I also seem to have slipped into a woman's body. In Paris, I am pretty sure I am a man, similar to my ordinary self except for the shoes. It's been said that to understand another person, you must walk in their shoes. I am a man who loves women, and is indeed surrounded by them, but I confess that there are many things about women I don't understand, including their special relationship with shoes.

My personal dream-production team, possibly supervised by a committee of goddesses, has subjected me to remedial education.

Do women dream of having four husbands? Please come inside my dream and form your own conclusions.

Her name is Doris. I don't think I ever met a woman with that name before, except on the screen, and she is nothing like Doris Day. Long, wavy, chestnut hair, attractive in a rangy, loose-boned way, well-suited by her flowing blouse, the kind that knots at the waist. She says her mother has started talking about dreams.

"Mom said she went flying, over the ocean, like a seagull. She flew further than she could say. She didn't know where she went, but she came back happy."

"That's a great dream for someone who might be getting ready to fly off from this world."

Doris bites her lip, just a little. I am worried I upset her. Though I did not mention the word *death*, she knows what I meant.

"Of course, your mom's probably got another good twenty years ahead." I feel like an awkward fool as soon as the words are out.

"Can we talk outside?"

It's a great idea. It's lovely outside, in the clearing, under the dappled light falling through the trees. I am a little nervous about what Doris is going to say, but it turns out to be fine. She wants to talk dreams, and we have an agreed method for doing that — something that gives you a handrail that will keep you fairly safe even when you are on the edge of a chasm of possible emotion and misunderstanding.

"You first," she prompts me.

I tell her a dream about a red fox, a lord who is under a curse, and a beautiful woman everyone wants to bed. There are plenty of scene shifts, unexplained jumps from one place or time to another.

"Are all your dreams as jumpy as this?"

"I often find myself asking, *How did I get here?*"

"Inside the dreams, or after?"

"Mostly after. But when I say that inside a dream, things get interesting."

"How so?"

"I become aware that I'm not on ordinary ground."

"So you become lucid? You're now in a lucid dream?"

"I don't always say to myself, *I must be dreaming.* You see, the scenes are usually completely real. I may say to people around me, *How did I get here?*"

"How do they respond?"

"Sometimes they look at me like I'm a nut. Sometimes they don't seem to see or hear me at all."

"What do you want to do with your dream?"

"I guess I can make more of a story out of it. Sometimes I feel that that's the best thing to do with a dream, even what the dream wants. To become a story."

"I like that idea."

"Do you have a story for me?"

"Sure, but let me go to the restroom first."

I watch her walk back to the lodge. The way she swings her hips, just enough, makes it clear she knows I am looking. I notice her shoes for the first time. They are red, and they have two-inch heels, almost too high for a country retreat at a place with wood-chip trails, certainly high enough to affirm her gender. I'm still slow to take in shoes. There is a difference between men and women.

With that thought, I decide to take a leak the boy's way. I walk between the trees to another clearing.

I stand in tall grass, looking out over a valley. Far in the distance is a farm I don't remember seeing before. From this remove, the people and animals are smaller than figures in a model railroad set. There is a horse, some sheep or goats, cows further off, in a meadow.

I unzip my jeans. If anyone is looking from over there, they'll miss the action.

I'm about to let go when something lets go of *me*.

I'm in a large, comfortably furnished family room. I don't know how I got here. Is this the farm I was looking at from the other side of the valley?

They are very relaxed, not surprised to see me. Seated together on a long sofa in front of a long table are three men and a woman. They appear to be about the same age, which could be anywhere from the mid-forties to well-preserved early sixties. One of the men is a little plumper than the others, but they could all be played by George Clooney. They match. So does the woman, smartly dressed in sensible country clothes, her dark hair up in a bun.

They welcome me to their home. They have been playing a board game — no, it is a rather complex jigsaw puzzle. The picture is one of those Escher-type things where staircases wind in and around each other and people seem to be walking on the ceiling.

The men shake hands with me one by one as the lady makes introductions. Raymond is sharp-eyed and correct, eyes glinting behind his wire-rimmed glasses. He does the numbers and fixes the computers and connections. Ranulph is the dreamer, smiling at his own thoughts, able to quote poems about anything, or make them up from the ordinary materials of life. Renato is the dessert chef, and you don't want any chef to be thin.

They sit down again in synchronized motion.

I know there's a fourth one. This lady has four husbands. As in any good court, there is always a Favorite. This position changes with her moods and her requirements. The Favorite is given special treats and special favors in the lady's bedroom, though the choice of activity and its postures are entirely at her discretion.

She has chosen her men to provide for all her needs — spiritual, mental, emotional, sexual. Having despaired of finding a single life partner who could serve her to her satisfaction on all levels, she has divided the job between four specialists.

I want to know how this works. She invites me to accompany her and Renato into the kitchen, which is beautifully equipped. She tells her husband she is in the mood for crème brûlée. In an instant, he is dressed in a white uniform with a high white chef's hat. Ingredients and implements fly to his hands. He is making magic in a white ceramic bowl. He is speaking of how it is of the earth, strengthened by fire, rounded like a woman's breast. As he prepares the dish, he explains, the clay of the bowl absorbs some of the heat, as the power of the flame dissolves the sugar on the surface of the cream and a delicate crust is created.

"Breaking the crust, my love, is like stripping your legs of silk stockings, ever so slowly, as I admire the beauty of your thighs, your calves, the grace of your tiny feet. When you break the crust, you feel the fire inside you and the heat of my desire. You dip your spoon into the smoothest cream. It is exactly the temperature of your body, under your creamy skin."

She is breaking the crust and dipping a teaspoon into what is beneath. I did not even see him put the bowl in the oven. This is truly a kitchen wizard.

"The taste in your mouth makes you close your eyes. You let yourself sink into a vanilla dream. It melts on your tongue. It brings alive all the cells of your body."

She seems to be panting as he goes on. "You feel your perfect lover is running his fingers gently over your spine, almost touching, but not quite yet. Teasing, flattering. You long for more. You take another teaspoon. All the papillae on your tongue are now awake and quivering. All your senses are alive."

The noises she is making now are orgasmic, embarrassing.

Do I get it? I understand that he knows things about crème brûlée that I do not. I am willing to yield the chef's hat to him.

He looks like a happy pig when she busses him on the cheek. Something is missing from this scene. The fourth husband.

There is a crash from the back of the house. I am there before the others, eager to see. A man browned and weathered by sun and wind, bare-chested under his dungarees, is laying down his tools in a screened porch that looks like a mudroom. An ax, a long-handled hammer, something that might be a plow.

"Randy," he offers a firm hand.

"Of course you are."

This must be the fourth husband. He looks much like the others, but thirty pounds lighter than Renato, and with muscle where Raymond has calculators.

The lady of the house kisses him full on the mouth. He says he'll take a shower.

"Later," she tells him. "I like you smelling of horses and leather. I'm ready for you now."

I fall out of the scene. For a moment, it is completely gone. I listen to the sound of trash collection in the street. I rub my eyes, disappointed that I have nothing from the night, no trace of the Traveler. Then, in an instant, the sequence returns: talking dreams under the trees, going to take a piss, the woman with four husbands.

Where was I — who was I — in the last scene?

Only a woman, surely, would dream of having four husbands as some kind of earthly paradise.

Doris didn't tell me a dream before we parted company. Did she somehow succeed in pulling me into one of her dreams?

I remember now that yesterday, tracking the Traveler, I noticed that I was wearing high-heeled shoes in an adventure in Paris. Was I a woman in that dream? In the dream of the woman with four husbands, was I my normal self, observing, or had I entered the consciousness and maybe the body of a woman, of Doris or a female version of myself?

Who is Doris anyway?

When the men spilling garbage cans on the street yanked me out of my adventure, did they bring me back to a world that is more real, or less real, than that of Doris or the woman with four husbands?

I talk to a woman I trust. I ask, "Do women have dreams of having many husbands?"

"Draupadi. She had five."

I know the name from a Hindu epic, the Mahabharata. I watched a film version but fell asleep.

"Five husbands? That's one up on my lady. How did Draupadi's guys get along together?"

"I think they had other wives."

"That's polyandry plus polygyny."

"If you say so."

"I'm asking about women today, not Hindu epics. Do women dream of having several husbands at the same time?"

"I'm not telling. But I once heard one girl say that if she could have her wish, she would have as many men on call as could satisfy her on every level."

"The Right Brothers instead of Mister Right."

I am trying to be clever, but I don't feel clever at all. I don't know what was going on with Doris and the lady with four husbands, but I do know this: I have made women my study, but I still don't know what they want.

How Much Ephesus Have You Had?

The famous Greek dream interpreter Artemidorus, who read dreams at Ephesus, wrote that "a wild boar signifies a violent storm for people traveling either by land or sea.... There is nothing strange in that, if the wild boar also signifies a woman."* The storm is greater when the woman is a goddess. The boar has a special association with Artemis. In the old stories, she sends a boar to punish men who offend her. She sent the famous Calydonian boar to ravage a kingdom whose ruler caused offense by failing to set a special place for her at a feast.

Vocatus atque non vocatus, deus aderit. "Invoked or uninvoked, the god is present." Jung carved these words in stone above his door. Gods happen. Goddesses happen even more. Especially when you speak as if they can't hear you.

---

* Artemidorus of Daldis, *Oneirocritica: The Interpretation of Dreams*, trans. Robert J. White (Torrance, CA: Original Books, 1990), 105–6.

"Don't you think there might be consequences for waking up the old gods?" my Dutch friend asked.

We were facing the sun inside the still-tremendous walls of the inner sanctuary of Apollo at his temple at Didyma. I had just led a chant, in ancient Greek, to awaken Apollo as Paian, the All-Healer. Curious German tourists took photographs.

Like a fool, I said to Aad, "Oh, they are family."

My mythic trouble might have started there. But I think its seeds were sown earlier, in Istanbul, and its spectacular serial crisis lay in the future, when forces of the deeper world erupted into the Anatolian day.

It may have started on the first afternoon in Sultanahmet, when a cheeky sidewalk vendor leaped from his perch to cry to us, "Am I the one you are looking for?" Or when we crested the steep street and I paused in front of the Blue Mosque to purchase fresh-squeezed pomegranate juice, tart and frothy. Pink slime stuck to my nose, and as Asli wiped it off, laughing, I joked that I was drinking the fruit that kept Persephone bound to Hades in the underworld, using god names loosely for the first time in a land where the old gods are easily aroused.

Or perhaps it began that first night in Istanbul. We parted in the hotel lobby, but Asli came to my room in her second body, fluttering her hands in the style of the native dancers, plucking possibilities from the night air, which she infused with smoky sweetness. She was not the only feminine presence in my room that night.

Snaking ahead of her was a creature of beauty and terror who tempted me with her flexible body and dared me to look into her drowned eyes. She flirted with me with her many tendrils and — putting on the face of a beautiful young woman — assured me that she had been given a bad rap by men. *I am not what they say I am. I am poison but I am medicine. I raise the serpent energy in men. When I turn men to stone, it means that I make them firm as rock.* Medusa as a sex goddess? I was not convinced. I tried to avoid looking directly into those dead eyes, which called me down to the bottom of a sunless sea. But I forgot to hold up the mirror that saved Perseus.

In the hour before dawn, I listened to the city's many layers of awakening. The roosters were first, followed by the rattle of trains, the murmur of doves, boat horns on the Bosporus, the hard conversation of crows. Then the *ezan*, the muezzin's call to prayer, repeated from one minaret to another, completing a circle of sound.

We met for breakfast among the ruins of the Grand Palace. I was surprised that Turkish coffee was not immediately on offer, and she gave me one of my first words of Turkish. Breakfast is called *kahvate*, which means "below coffee." Turks drink tea at breakfast, coffee later, inverting Western expectations. The best tea, she explained, is "rabbit's blood," red and clear. I ate olives and tomatoes with goat cheese and crusty bread, and we peeled fresh figs. She gave no sign that she was aware that she had come to my room in the night, in her second body, and I did not embarrass her with my recollections.

We flew to Izmir and met the rest of our party: Aad, a Dutch therapist I had met at conferences, and Oana, a young Romanian archaeologist. Professor Semander had personally selected us for this trip. The only thing he would say about his purposes was that we were all in need of a holiday. He had arranged for us to visit a series of sites along the Ionian coast that were sacred to the Greeks. To my surprise, Semander had decided to abstract himself from the tour at the last minute, hinting that he had found the tracks of an ancient order of female dervishes. He gave me strict instructions to meet him at the apartment he had rented or borrowed in Ortaköy on my return from the south. As always, he expected a full report.

We agree in Izmir that we will start at the precinct of Apollo. The columns of his fallen temple at Didyma still stand tall against the sky. At the gate of the precinct are three Medusa heads; be careful how you go here. We walk past stone lions and carved bull's heads and mount the steps of the outer temple.

The walls of the inner temple are only a third their original size, but still rise high above us as we go down toward the sacred spring, where the oracle once sang through the vocal cords of an inspired prophetess.

Blessedly, there are few tourists at the temple today. Shall I call to him? I decide to take the risk.

In the inner temple, facing the sun, I join hands with the friends who have come with me on this tour of Ionian temples. I lead the singing in Greek

Egreio Apollon!

Egreio Paian!

Arise, Apollo!

Arise, All-Healer!

Some curious German visitors snap pictures. The words reverberate across the enclosure. Sound must have been an essential part of the rituals conducted here. The acoustics are still extraordinary.

I am drinking the sun, filling with light and music.

We sit near the place of the oracle. It is then that Aad asks, "Don't you think there may be consequences for awakening old gods?"

My response — "Oh, they are family" — is inexcusable in someone who knows anything of the family life of the old gods. To declare them family is not only an act of hubris, but an invitation for ancient dramas of jealousy and passion and hate to irrupt into present lives. If I had overheard someone else doing this, I might have said: you just invited mythic trouble.

A sweet, long-haired redhead — one of the stray dogs you see everywhere in these parts — comes to nuzzle me and lick me, and this feels like a blessing. Pilgrims at the temples of dream healing were always hoping for friendly encounters with dogs.

Oana asks, "What do you think went on here in ancient times?"

I hear great waves of sound, choral voices, musicians. Sound was all-important in the rites celebrated here.

I see a giant statue of Apollo at the center of the precinct. On his shoulders appear twin birds, black and white. They are both ravens. Of course: ravens were the birds of Apollo, and his seers use their sight very much as Odin does.

Oana agrees. Bird watching was a vital part of divination here. We imagine looking through ancient eyes that quartered the sky and attributed different contexts and different outcomes to the behavior of birds in each of these segments.

We leave Apollo's temple and drive to a little museum at Miletus, where we study a map that shows the route of those who started from here along the Sacred Way. They began by making a payoff to a dark and fierce goddess of crossroads, Hecate. I have made no offering. I drop a coin outside the door, doubtful that this will suffice.

A winding coast road brings us to Karina and an open-air restaurant on a little cove. It is very hot and humid under awnings that fail to keep off the sun, and no-see-ums are soon trying to eat my face. The restaurant is deserted except for the waiters and an odd monkeylike man who stares hard at us. The fresh catch, we are told, is squid or sea bass; I opt for the bass, and the local beer, Efes, which is Ephesus in Turkish. When the bread and appetizers arrive, we are petitioned by rival families of ducks, gray and brown. They are very aggressive beggars, crying for more before they finish swallowing the first offerings.

Beyond the restaurant, the road ends at a little naval station, where Turks glare at the Greeks on Samos across the narrow strait, and they all watch for refugees from the Middle East trying to get into Europe. Dinghies and fishing boats bob in the water.

I am stunned to see a capuchin monkey scampering between the tables. Where did he come from?

"There's a monkey in the restaurant!" I tell my companions.

"How much Ephesus have you had?" Asli asks. Her back is turned to the monkey.

"See for yourself."

She turns, as do the others, and they are amazed.

The monkey vanishes but reappears, this time in a harness and leash held by the monkeylike man, as I am engaged in stripping fish from the bones. With that same hard stare, his intentions obscure, the monkey man advances to our table. He allows the monkey to grab for Aad's plate and then climb Asli's arm and start to maul her. We protest. He is in no hurry to take the monkey away, but does so when the waiter returns.

"What's the story with the monkey?" I ask the waiter.

He shrugs and walks away, but returns later to tell us that the monkey belongs to this place; he was raised here. The monkey man does not belong; he is a Bulgarian odd-job man they think is weird. The message, we agreed at the table, was, *Watch out for monkey business.* But I had forgotten it by the time we reached Ephesus.

We walk the ruins of the colossal temple city. I don't much like it, with all its accretions of megalomaniac emperors and commercial avarice. The heat is terrible, and we risk constant collision with sun-drunk mobs of tourists lurching after upraised umbrellas and pennants. I like the cats sprawled everywhere on broken columns and pediments. I take a photo of another Medusa. I do not climb up the stone seats in the great ancient theater, or visit the remains of the brothels.

We drive to Selçuk, to the museum of Ephesus. And there, in a moment of casual and reckless jest, I learn the consequences of proclaiming that old gods are family.

Through the entrance hall, up a few steps, I turn to my right and see a life-sized statue of the celebrated goddess of many breasts, Artemis of Ephesus. She is younger and prettier than I expected. I admire her for a long time, wondering whether all those dangling protuberances around her torso are little breasts or something else — figs, perhaps, or eggs. She wears the zodiac as her necklace.

I feel a prickling at the back of my neck. I turn to face a larger, elder, sterner version of the Great Goddess of Ephesus. She wears a city as her crown, and many animals are in her train.

I turn back to the prettier, younger image. I make a little bow, and announce to my friends, "This is the lady I'll ask out to dinner."

Nobody laughs. Asli is horrified. "Do you have any idea what you are doing?" Her passport says she is Muslim. Her lifestyle says she is part of the cosmopolitan, essentially secular intelligentsia of Istanbul, the bicontinental city. But she is also a woman of Anatolia, the land of a thousand deities, where the wisdom of the simple people is that you try to avoid offending any of the ones that may be listening.

I have just slighted the elder Artemis. There she is, standing tall in the breathing image that was worshipped and infused with power by millions of people over many centuries. There is no glass between us.

I feel a little ripple of concern, but it is transient, like a little cold water underfoot in the bathtub when you start running the shower. It is gone before we step out into the heat of the day, to drink Efes beer under the trees at a courtyard café.

After breakfast at the hotel, Asli turns over her coffee cup to read the grounds. She sees a pig and shudders. Pork is forbidden in her culture.

I want to swim in the Aegean. We agree to make a picnic. We pick up flat Turkish loaves, salami and cheese, yogurt and olives, and of course Ephesus beer. We drive to İçmeler, a beach in a national park. As we walk through the trees to the white sandy beach, I am startled to see large brown animals in the woods.

"Wild boars," Asli confirms. "Don't worry about them. They've been here forever, and they never bother anyone."

This seems evident. Turkish families at picnic tables under the trees are paying no attention to the boars. We claim a free table in the shade. I take off my shirt and start making a salami sandwich. I sense a stir of movement behind me. I turn and see a boar that is rushing toward me. I decide to adopt the casual local attitude. I return to fixing my sandwich, tearing off a strip of bread I may throw to the boar, the same way I've been feeding stray dogs.

The boar has a different idea. It sinks its teeth into my lower back, over the left kidney.

Turks at the neighboring tables jump up, amazed and aghast. Blood pouring from the hole in my back, I spin round to face the boar. It is running at me again, fast and direct. I grab my sandal and brandish it. I thwack it against the table, and the boar swerves away. But four or five more have gathered. A Turkish woman appears with a long stick and plays guardian, pushing the boars back.

There is a Turkish doctor at a nearby table. He takes a quick look at the hole in my back and tells me to wash the wound with soap and water and get to a pharmacy for iodine and bandages and antibiotics. I am fortunate, he tells me, that the boars here aren't rabid. But a tetanus shot might be a good idea. His wife gives me a little bar of soap. They tell me, "You are very unusual."

I am not in pain, though the hole in my back seems huge and blood is streaming down my back and pooling in the sand. Dazed and dreamy, I am also hungry. I devour some bread and salami, and am surprised by how good it tastes. The others want to get me to a pharmacy. I insist on getting into the Aegean first. I came here to swim in Homer's wine-dark sea, and this is what I will do.

It's low tide, and I must walk far out before I can swim. People are gawking at the blood streaming down my back. I reassure myself with the thought that salt water has always been a great cleanser.

When we come out of the sea, I want to stay on the beach and drink Ephesus. Aad shrugs. It's up to me, and he's ready for a beer. We rent loungers and I stretch out, bleeding into a hotel towel. Oana lights a cigarette and starts reading a novel in French. I light a cigar. Through the haze, I see the boars watching us from the edge of the woods.

As we prepare to leave the beach, a bee lands on my right arm, seemingly with deliberation, and plants its stinger. The bee falls to the sand. I remove the stinger and say, "I got my shot." This feels like a positive intervention. I want to give thanks to another goddess, the one who works with the bees and the bee priestesses. Aad tells me that a bee sting would have mobilized my immune system, and helped.

As we start back to the car, the stubbly man who rents the beach recliners runs up. He has something to tell us. "I've worked here for twenty years," he explains to Asli, who translates. "I have never seen a boar attack anyone. This is not usual at all. Something very strange is going on."

At the *eczane* — drugstore — in town, they don't believe me when I tell them what happened. The people in the pharmacy think I am joking until I lift the back of my aloha shirt and show them the wound. When my friends apply iodine and bandages at the hotel, I finally see my physical condition clearly. There is a big red hole in my back and a smaller one above, surrounded by a livid purple bruise about a foot wide.

Asli phones my room that evening, with a warning. No, she won't visit me. But she needs to tell me she fears something terrible is about to happen. I must do my best to stay safe and call on protection.

I drink more Ephesus, and a little raki, before I drift into fitful sleep next to the horrible plug-in mosquito repellent that is the only alternative to being drained of blood. I surface at 4:00 AM feeling terrible. My inner sight is a chaos of dark and obscure images, scary things that refuse to settle into solid forms. I feel what I have heard described as vastation — absence of light, of guidance, of connection with higher powers, with the divine. For the first time on this odyssey, I know fear. I feel I could die here, in Anatolia. This is not in itself the source of fear — if I am to die, why not here? Rather, I am scared of being hurled into bardo realms without a compass or a guide. Who knew where I might find myself in an Anatolian afterlife, bereft of counsel and protection?

I recognize that I am like the cartoon character who notices that he has walked over a cliff only when he looks down and then starts to fall. I feel besieged by dark, chaotic, and implacable forces, by Furies bent on taking my life or driving me insane, in either order. Like a reckless, jesting boy, I have provoked the jealous rage of a goddess. In the myths, this rarely works out well for mortal men, and is known to start wars.

I see the scene in the museum at Ephesus again, through different eyes. Standing between two living goddesses, I turned my back on the elder and announced that I would take the younger and prettier one out to dinner. This would have pissed off any woman, but I had chosen to piss off the Great Goddess of Anatolia, the worst of all female powers to rouse to anger. Many-breasted Artemis of Ephesus is also Cybele, perhaps the scariest of all goddesses to men, and one whose story — in my plumbing of myths — I had preferred to avoid. She flies into a frenzy when she learns that her mortal lover has fallen for a mortal woman. In her frenzy, Cybele drives her lover, Attis, insane, and he cuts off his own balls. In her cult, the men who served her were eunuchs.

The attack of the wild boar is no longer a laughing matter. Had my back not been turned, its jaws might have closed on a more vulnerable part of my anatomy. I realize that in order to survive in this country, I must find a way to pacify a wrathful goddess. I am quite certain that I can never return to Anatolia without doing this and might not even manage to leave.

I must make amends to the Great Goddess, and whatever I am going to do must be done now, while I am on the land where I had offended her. I must stop myself from trying to figure things out and ask for help from whatever friendly powers might take an interest in my cause. I say out loud, "I have been a silly boy. Help me to make amends."

As my vision clears, I see the Goddess in three approachable forms. I see her as the deep, loamy body of Earth and remember how I had offered bread and beer to her in other landscapes, returning the gifts of the Mother to the Mother. I see a dear sister who walks close to Mary, reminding me gently that Mary is the Goddess in her most benign and merciful form, incorporating previous forms. We grow our gods, and our goddesses, and I should speak to the Goddess in her higher evolution. I see the owl eyes of Athena. When I once found myself contending with chthonic and chaotic forces on a journey to the Lower World, she loaned me owl eyes of wisdom that glowed in the dark places like twin lanterns.

A plan begins to form. I will take bread and beer, gifts of the Earth Goddess, and offer them at the gates of the Ephesus temple. I will go to the House of Mary, near Ephesus, where the mother of Jesus supposedly lived for the last years of her life, brought here by John the apostle; the exact location, atop a mountain, was discovered by a German nun in a dream. And I will go to the temple of Athena in the mountains, at Priene.

I am excited to tell Asli my plan when we meet with the others in the morning. Asli points out that a key element is missing. "You must speak to the Goddess at the museum where you offended her." The others agree. This is scary, but I accept that it must be done.

We return to Ephesus. We go first to the entrance to the temple complex, where we wheedle an attendant into letting us park for a few minutes among the tourist coaches on the pretext that I am going to buy water at the busy market area in front of the turnstiles. There is no good place to leave bread and pour beer right in front of the gates — not an inch of grass or raw earth — so I place the loaves at the base of a tree standing in its own little patch of earth in the middle of the concourse. I pour Efes for Efes, Ephesus beer for the Lady of Ephesus, asking humbly that my offering should be accepted.

"*Tamam*," Asli says when I go back to the car. "That's okay for now, but next time you want to offer bread in my country you must place it up high, for the birds. Bread is precious."

It's time to confront the Lady herself. I am feeling a little skittish about talking to the Elder Goddess I insulted. The museum is strangely empty of tourists. I feel as if the space has been cleared for the encounter that is about to take place. In the room of the goddesses, a female custodian sits silent, eyes down, between the younger and the elder Artemis.

I look again at those rows of tiny breasts around the torso of Artemis. They remind me of something else. Could they be balls? If they are testicles, they are not from *l'homme moyen sensuel*. They are the balls of wild bulls, or mythic heroes. This is not a cheering thought. I wince, remembering how the Great Goddess of Anatolia punished her errant lover, Attis, by driving him crazy so that he castrated himself. I feel a painful twinge in a private place and see clearly what would have happened had I not turned my back the moment the wild boar at the beach tried to make me a ham sandwich.

I stand before the breathing image of Artemis. I bow my head. I say, "I am a silly boy, reckless and passionate and unreflective. I failed to give you the honor and respect you deserve. I come to make amends. I hope you will accept my apology, and my humble offerings."

There is something more I need to add. "I offer you —"

I am about to say, "my love," but an instinct of survival restrains. "My love" could be construed to include my genitals. No, I do not offer my love, but "my respect. My creativity. My best words, to write and sing your story and to honor all women, and the Goddess in all women."

Aad, embarrassed, walks off to look at other things in the museum. Oana goes outside for a cigarette.

I repeat myself in front of the Goddess with a city in her hair. I know I sound desperate. The carved face of the Elder Goddess is unyielding, implacable. I call myself a silly boy yet again. Asli says, "I saw her smile."

I don't see it.

"Just a little smile. Less than Mona Lisa. But yes, a smile."

"You're sure?"

"Yes, I'm sure. This is done. She's letting you go this time."

She reminds me to speak to the younger Artemis also. No goddess should be made to feel slighted. Even though I have been humbled, I have to stop myself blowing a kiss to the younger of the many-breasted goddesses.

It's not all done. I made promises to three forms of the Goddess. Keeping the next promise requires me to take the steep, winding road to the House of Mary, on Mount Nightingale, Bülbüldağı. The visions of a Catholic nun in another country revealed a stone house on this mountain as the last home of Mary, the name of the Goddess recognized by the church. The church has not ruled on whether Sister Catherine's visions were true, but it is happy for the faithful to come here with their prayers and petitions and contributions.

Japanese tourists are taking group selfies in front of a wishing wall festooned with prayers for intercession written on pieces of paper, tightly rolled or wadded. I wonder what they know of Mary. Perhaps they see her as the sister of their own merciful goddess, Kwan Yin.

I pray in Mary's chapel and drink the waters of her spring. I light a candle on a terrace overlooking Ephesus, cupping my hands to prevent it from being extinguished by the changeable mountain winds.

There is a third promise to keep. We drive to Priene and climb the high stone steps to the ruined temple of Athena. I drink in fresh, strong wind and look over a vast panorama of meadows and farmlands with delight. The pitted mountain rising above the columns of the temple feels like an old friend. I am entirely at home here, and I am blessed.

I speak to Athena as Sophia, as the Divine Feminine Wisdom. I feel inner certainty that she is with me.

In the twilight, we walk the Kordon in Izmir, enjoying the extraordinary sea breeze of this part of the coast. Asli says, "Those of us who live in Anatolia know we are surrounded by gods and spirits. Whatever our beliefs, we step around the gods carefully. We respect them and don't stir them up. This time you invited the fury of the boar that nobody has seen attack humans in modern times. Next time you could attract the Anatolian leopard, which nobody has seen in generations."

"I think I would rather take my chances with the leopard than the boar."

At the airport, a very tall and big-boned Teutonic woman is ordering about a party of ladies of only slightly lesser stature, who are wearing sensible shoes. I can't resist joking that her mustache suits the drill-sergeant role she is playing.

Asli punches my arm, not gently. "What are you thinking of? How do you know there isn't a Goddess of Women with Mustaches?"

Professor Semander has given me an address, and I have a report to make. Could the taxi driver have picked a longer route through the roiling traffic of the vast city of Istanbul? It is raining hard by the time he bumps to a halt at a street market in Ortaköy. I look out at a warren of stalls loaded with jewelry, fabrics, and tourist knickknacks. There must be some mistake. But the driver jumps out and hoists my suitcase onto his back. "*Hati, Hati!* Quick! Quick!" I run after him, trying not to slip on the wet pavement. He leads me on a crazy zigzag path among the crowded alleys before he stops at the door of a shop offering beads and tattoos.

He hands my bag to a boy and accepts the bills I give him, and I follow my suitcase, bouncing on a second back, upstairs.

Semander receives me on a terrace overlooking the Bosporus and the suspension bridge between Europe and Asia. He loves edgy places. To the left of the terrace, we look down at the courtyard of a mosque. Semander pours both of us wine — forbidden to the faithful — and raises his glass to the mosque before he clinks mine.

"You really were a silly boy. You got off lightly. Odysseus bore the mark of a boar's tusk on his inner thigh. No prizes for guessing how he earned *that. Polytropos*, polyamorous. The man of many ways and many women."

He contemplates the winking lights of the party boats and cruise ships on the Bosporus, where the current flows both ways.

"Humans are such forgetful animals. None more forgetful than a man when his wick is lit. You must remember the story of the Calydonian Boar."

I searched my schoolboy memories. "One of the labors of Hercules," I venture.

"That's not the point of the story, not for *you*. The holy terror of a giant boar was loosed on the people of Calydon when their king forgot to include Artemis in the gods to whom he made offerings at a festival of first fruits. The goddess felt slighted, of course. In her wrath, she unleashed the most savage of her animal familiars. The name of the forgetful king, by the way, was Oenus. The Wine Man. There is something for you in that too.

"It took the hand of a woman to bring down the boar of Artemis on that occasion. It was Atalanta who struck that mother of all pigs with an arrow. Just a glancing blow, but painful. Then the heroes got their chance and Meleager, son of the Wine Man, got in the coup de grâce. How is this resonating with you?"

"It does."

"Perhaps it's not a bad thing that, like wandering Odysseus — another favorite of Athena — you'll carry the mark of the boar. We can't afford to forget what can happen in a life when we fall over a mythic edge. Gods happen. Goddesses happen, and sometimes they bite. We heard that Great Pan is dead; we said that we are modern and scientific and free from a universe haunted by gods, demons, and others. Yet the myths live on; the Goddess rises again.

"Jung knew this well in his own life. He compared the force of a myth that is rising again to what happens in a dry creek bed when a tempest blows up and turns it into a raging torrent. I assume you read his paper 'The Psychology of the Child Archetype.' Yes? Well, read it again. What he says there is essential: we cannot *explain* or dispose of an archetype. The most we can do is dream the myth onwards and give it modern dress.

"You do this without thinking about it. That's your story with the boar and the Goddess. That's why you are a poster boy for mythic trouble. You dream the myth onwards and give it modern dress without noticing what you are doing. What you must do — *everything*, for you, may depend on this — is become lucid within the dream you are living day and night."

The Other Novelist

Have you encountered a parallel self who is having a really good time on another event track? Have you ever wanted to step into their place? That is not straightforward, in the many worlds.

I find a gap in the traffic and hurry across the sidewalk, up the great marble steps of the library. The lions that flank the steps are glowing gold in the late sun. The effect is astonishing. They really seem to be gold instead of stone. I would like to touch them to correct this illusion, but I am running late.

The security guards don't bother with me. This is natural; the event is in my honor and they must have recognized me from my photographs.

The reception is lively and well-lubricated. I recognize actors and entrepreneurs, models and editors, and of course many of the city's literary lions. I reach for a champagne flute from the tray of a passing waiter. He skates by as if I don't exist, which is ruder than I would expect, even in a city renowned for acerbic behavior.

I glance up at the posters that fill the walls. They have been produced and hung especially for this occasion. They are blowups of the covers of my books. It's strange that I don't recognize the artwork. Have my publishers produced new jacket designs without consulting me? Stranger still, I don't recognize some of the titles. I am relieved to find a familiar title among the displays. *The Blue World.* But again, the cover art is new to me.

The flying waiter reappears, with freshly charged glasses. I leap at him, determined to get a drink. I realize I am going to bump into him, and try to adjust my attack. The waiter quivers, the champagne sloshes over the edges of the glasses, but there is no collision. He stops and looks around, frowning. "Sorry," I say to him, "I'm just rather thirsty."

He does not acknowledge me. When I reach for a glass again, he rushes away, leaving me parched.

My attention is diverted because I recognize a publisher with whom I had major business decades ago. He looks as self-important as ever, though I know he must now take his orders from a multimedia corporation for which book publishing is less important than reality TV. I call out a greeting, and he cuts me dead. Surely he's not holding on to old rancors. I try again, offering a jesting remark. He goes on chatting with a pair of socialites as if I do not exist.

I hear my name being spoken over the public-address system. My lecture is due to begin. Guests are invited to take their seats immediately, because the event is overbooked.

When I enter the auditorium, I am intrigued to see droves of children as well as adults, some seated with their families, some in excited groups, perhaps part of school or club outings. Many of them have piles of books on their laps, evidently hoping for autographs. I try to identify the books, peering over young shoulders.

My name is on all the books, but the titles and cover designs, again, are strange to me.

Someone is testing the microphone. There is brief applause for the publisher who ignored me earlier. He calls me "our beloved storyteller." He quotes numbers — millions of copies sold, weeks on bestseller lists — and gets wild applause from the sales reps seated on the right side of the room.

He gives a little of my biography. Now he is welcoming me to the stage. I rush toward the platform.

The applause is deafening. I am thrilled by the laughing, beaming faces of the children. When did my books become so popular with them? I delight in the glowing faces of the women.

I march toward the podium, my arm outstretched to give a handshake to the publisher, who can't ignore me now. But someone is there ahead of me. Broad-shouldered, wearing a tweed jacket like mine, with longish white hair like mine, but better-groomed. I scan him from top to bottom. His pants are better-cut than mine, his shoes are hand-tooled English brogues instead of mud-spattered sneakers, and he is wearing a tie.

He turns to his audience, and I see his profile. It is my own, just a little tighter and more tanned, as if he has just returned from an elegant second home on the ocean.

Suddenly I understand what is going on. I've been wandering around in a dream, confusing the experiences I am having in my dream body with what is happening with my real self, in its physical body, in the real world. I am a dissociated part of myself, a part that doesn't recognize everything that has been going on in the real world because I lost track of myself. All will be well if I just get back into the solid body up there on the stage. When I do this, I will enjoy, with him, the fruits of all his success. I will no longer be a ghost at my own party. And of course I will know exactly what to say on the podium, in front of those microphones and cameras and excited faces.

I drift up behind the speaker. It seems to me that the right place to enter him is at the base of the neck. I read somewhere that wizards call this the *soul gate*. I make it my intention to become small enough to slip in. I will then expand inside him to merge with his mind and his vital organs.

As quick as thought, I am in. I am seeking a mind lock. But something resists me. Inside the speaker's body, he is fighting to possess himself, and he is stronger. "*Get out*," he snarls at me. "Go away. You are too late."

I have to respect him, because it comes to me now that he is *other*. He is living a life I departed many years ago, when I abandoned the novel called *The Blue World*. Had I persisted, its popularity would have brought publishers competing to publish sequel after sequel, winning an avid world audience of children and young adults as well as older readers.

I must go back to the life I have been living in a similar, yet quite different reality, one of the many parallel worlds of the multiverse.

"Too late," he cries after me, as I flee the library.

But is it truly too late to pick up some of the threads of what I allowed to unravel, and bring something from the life of the other novelist into my life?

Heaven and Earth

Have you sensed that you may be living more than one life right now? The many-worlds hypothesis in physics suggests that you have doppelgangers leading parallel lives in innumerable parallel worlds. Have you dreamed you are living in a different place, with a different partner, and the story moves forward in dream after dream, like a television series? Those serial dreams may be memories of a continuous life you are leading in a parallel reality. In the dream of waking life, the distance between you and an alternate self might be exactly as long as a hopscotch board.

The change in Mikey was amazing. She would have to remember to stop calling him that. He was no longer Mikey, or Mike, or even Michael. He was Mihai. He said his mother had wanted to give him that name, but the family thought it would get him teased and bullied in school. It was an old family name from his mother's country, and the name, he told her, of their national poet.

Its strangeness suited him; so did the link to a poet. Mihai had always had poetry in him. She remembered the awkward verses he had written for her in high school, and how he had left them, anonymously, in a tightly wadded page on her desk, too shy to even write his name. She unfolded the paper and read:

> You who move so surely
> I could love you like a puma
> Love you and make you wholly
> Tiger cat and woman.

This made her blush, but not to the roots of her hair, the way that he blushed when she grazed against him in the cafeteria line and whispered, "So when are you going to show me what you know about pumas?"

He avoided her completely for a couple of days after that. But in the night, she felt something in her room, something like a boy and something like a big cat. It nuzzled against her. She did not resist, because it gave her pleasure, touching her where she had not allowed anyone to touch her.

She decided to do something about this. She asked Mikey — not yet Mihai — out. For a picnic by the river. They talked and ate sandwiches, and she got in the swing in the children's playground and went so high that he begged her to stop. He read more poetry to her, some of his own, but mostly from dead poets with Irish and French and Eastern European names. He was very good-looking, in a slightly girly-boy way. She allowed him to make a first attempt on her virginity, but that did not go well. He did not seem to know what to do with her body, or his own. In his ordinary skin — still subject to breakouts — he was not the cat man who had given her a full-body orgasm in the night.

And he did not seem to know how to walk in the world. He was vague about what he was going to do at college and what he would do afterward. So she began to move away, to a guy on the football team who had been asking her out for months and was voted by the girls in her class as the hottest boy in school.

But this transit from Mikey to Mihai canceled out sour memories — of the failed first attempt under a tree, of the jock who broke her open like a battering ram, of a conventional marriage and banquets with overstuffed car dealers and a country-club life. They weren't ready when they were kids, but they were ready now. This was their time. Mihai was even more romantic, if that was possible, than the moony teen who had told her, in the voice of a dead Irish poet, that he had spread his dreams under her feet. And Mihai was worldly at the same time. He knew how to talk to concierges and headwaiters. He always got them on the right line on the Metro, where they rode past stations with names out of a fantasy bodice ripper: Sèvres-Babylone, Château d'Eau, Opéra. He knew museums where the statues seemed to live and breathe. He whisked her into discreet restaurants off the tourist track, where every dish, from the amuse-bouche to the climactic *café gourmand* or crème brûlée, pampered her senses and prepared her for love. His pockets were filled with cash. It seemed his books were doing very well.

What better partner for a visit to the city of lovers?

The only shadow on her glorious day was cast by an irritating dream, one of those ones that comes again and again. In the dream, she was back in an airless marriage, expected to dress up and play Stepford wife at tedious country-club dinners, and never to breathe a word of criticism against the Republicans in government. Nobody in that life knew about café gourmand or crème brûlée. Her husband was a big earner, so they had a house four times bigger than they needed, a condo in Florida, and several cars in the garage.

She did miss the kids. But wait a minute. She had left the

marriage, thank God, before they had kids. The kids were only in the dream that kept coming back. A lovely little girl with braids. A shy little boy who loved *Star Wars*. It was weird how real they seemed in the dream. This made her sad. It made her feel she was missing something in her life. She could not imagine having children with Mihai, of bringing diapers into their romance.

Why did she feel guilty?

She did not usually remember her dreams, but was starting to realize that some mornings she was carrying a hangover that had nothing to do with the wine drunk the previous evening. She shook her head and breathed in the spring air, trying to get out of the dream hangover.

She turned onto the Rue des Écoles. The traffic was light. Mihai had told her that this time of day — *entre cinq et sept heures* — was the preferred time for assignations in France. Her heart beat a little faster as she neared the place where they had agreed to meet. He had an appointment, he had told her. He suggested a café near the apartment where she could sip cappuccino and watch spring lovers go by.

"We'll meet at The Poet," he had said. The Poet was the other Mihai, the one revered in the country of his ancestors. He had been so excited to discover the statue here, on their very first promenade.

She had nothing to hide, nothing to hide from, yet she enjoyed the sense of covert intrigue as she neared the statue. It stood in a little apron of sidewalk too small to be called a courtyard. Children liked the pavement here, a smooth surface for drawing in chalk. The children were gone now, but they had left something behind: a hopscotch board.

She paused in front of the statue of the poet Mihai Eminescu. Bronze hair streaming, long coattails flapping in an invisible wind. The hopscotch board looked like the ones she remembered, except here, of course, the itinerary was in French. You start on *Terre*. If you're lucky, you get to *Ciel* before you turn around and have to hop back, if you can, to where you started.

This was irresistible. She reached in her purse for a coin she could use as a taw. She brought out a two-euro piece. Two concentric rings, the alloys looking like silver and gold. She turned it over in her hands. On the obverse she saw a primal image, something that might have been dug out of a Neolithic cave, and writing in Greek and some other language. Perhaps a goddess figurine. Was that a cross around her neck? No, it was a smaller image of herself. This seemed very strange. Well, the coin would have to do. Two euros, two goddesses. Double the luck.

Since she was playing herself, and had an appointment, she decided to skip the long succession of throws, starting with the rectangle numbered 1. She aimed at the 9, but failed to keep the coin inside the box. It landed on the line. She retrieved and tried again. A good throw. The coin was in the ninth box, and now she was hopping on one foot across the first squares, landing on two feet where she was meant to and — whooping with delight — she reached Heaven on both feet.

She turned around. Time to hop back to Earth. There. She was good, she was unstoppable.

"Mommy, Mommy!" a little girl yelled at her, making a face. "Mommy, you cheated!"

She gaped at the beautiful child with braids and cornflower-blue eyes, pouting a little, at the well-manicured lawn around the drive where they had painted a hopscotch board, at the rooftops of other McMansions in this gated development. She rubbed her eyes, then closed them. She was back in the dream in which she was a Stepford mom. The dream had come after her. Funny how a dream could do that. She willed herself back into her real life with Mihai in Paris.

She opened her eyes. The little girl — Felicity, she now remembered — had her hands on her hips.

"Daddy says you're always off in dreamland. Are you playing or not?"

"Yes, sweetie. Mommy's still in the game."

The Other Bollingen

Jung built a personal sanctuary near the village of Bollingen on the northern shore of Lake Zurich and called it his Tower. He was partly inspired by childhood fantasies of a castle on an island on a lake. Shortly before his death, Jung dreamed of the Other Bollingen, its counterpart in another world. The place was suffused with sourceless light. The deep voice he had come to trust told him that his new home had been completed and was now ready for him to move in.

Jung's biographer Barbara Hannah recalls that he had often dreamed of this Other Bollingen, in various stages of construction, and always understood that he was seeing a location on the Other Side of death. The new dream made it clear to her that he would soon be leaving to go to the Other Bollingen. "In fact," she writes, "it may have been this dream that loosened his strong tie to his earthly Bollingen."*

---

* Barbara Hannah, *Jung, His Life and Work: A Biographical Memoir* (Boston: Shambhala, 1991), 344.

1

A pleasant cemetery, with elegant headstones and family mausoleums, a place to walk the dogs and even picnic in the dappled light under ancient trees. I walk the rise, as I have done before, until I see the cabins on a slope below. They are just inside the boundary of the graveyard, but when I first discovered them I was amazed, because they are so unlike the other constructions here. They are brightly painted, in all kinds of color combinations: royal blue with canary-yellow trim, lime green with blood orange, hot pink and vanilla. The colors tickle the retinas, calling, "Party time!" Yet the voice I heard when I was first guided to this side of the cemetery was stern: *you must prepare your houses of death*.

When I first came to the cabins, I hardly hesitated before choosing the one for me: blue with yellow trim. The door opened easily. I found myself in a little room, empty of furniture except for a rocker that was still moving, as if someone had just got up from it. The far wall was missing. The view was completely open to a lovely cove with a curving white beach and a soft sea breeze. I was drawn to the water, of course, and found a lovely woman waiting for me. She stood waist-deep in the sea, sun-kissed, in something like a sarong, holding a conch shell to her ear. She kissed me lightly and offered the shell, motioning for me to hold it to my ear. When I did, I received a string of instructions for a sea crossing. I could take one of the dolphins — I saw them now, saddled like ponies — or a boat, or borrow the wings of a sea bird.

Across the waters, I saw the destination. An island shimmered on the horizon. A mist rolled in, and the island vanished. The mist moved on, and the island was revealed again. I knew what was waiting on that shore: a safe landing on the Other Side of death, perhaps a departed loved one or a welcoming committee. I made a journey that day, skimming the water like a cormorant, and met a dead poet who played guide to a realm that is now familiar to me, with all its possibilities of an ever-expanding life among schools and temples and pleasure palaces whose architects are creative imaginations.

I have brought many to the Houses of Death to prepare for their own passage.

Today I am playing the role of friendly guide again, walking a group through the cemetery, past the great family vaults and the headstones, to the blaze of colors down there on the slope. I wait until everyone in the group has made their choice and entered their own cabins before I return to my own: the little blue house with the yellow trim.

There are things I would like to do on the Other Side today. I would like to return to the apartment I made my own on previous visits. It has a rooftop terrace with a huge saltwater pool, framed by jasmine and honeysuckle. When I have swum enough there, I can walk to the edge of the terrace and dive into the bright blue waters of the bay below. The drop is twenty stories or more, but in the body I have over here, there is no risk of breaking my neck, or anything else. I plunge deep and swim underwater for a long time, without need to surface for air, until I am ready to fly up, like a bird. Sometimes I meet a lover in midair and we come together like mating eagles. When I have done with these sports, I go to my library and continue my studies. I have the same passion for research into all the byways of mind and soul that I have in my regular life, but here there is no interruption because of fatigue or blurring vision. I have a bed, but it is not for sleep. It is for love and creation. When I lie down with the intention of making a dream, images that engage my whole sensorium play around me on all sides. I am inside a holo-deck that is spontaneous, not mechanical.

I wonder whom I will meet today. Perhaps I will simply spend more time observing my other self, the one who left his physical body long ago and has been living and writing books on the Other Side. Maybe he will allow me to bring back some of his pages. This will obviously increase my speed of production when I peck at my keyboard in ordinary reality.

I approach the little blue house with joy and anticipation. The door opens smoothly, and I am inside. I am startled to find the room is not as I left it. There is a wooden stand to my left, with a pipe rack and jars of tobacco. Where did all these pipes come from? I experimented with a pipe when I was a student, wanting, no doubt, to look like a professor. But pipe smoking gave me a dry mouth, and in a temper I was liable to bite down on the stem so hard that it snapped. So pipes aren't much of my story.

I open a jar and sniff the tobacco. Too sweet for me, and not a brand that I know. Mystified, I turn toward the view through the open wall. This, too, has changed. I am looking across a lake, not the ocean. There is a wall at the lake's edge. Through mist along the shore, among light woods, I have the impression of a house with a tower. The scene is blurry, like my memory of a postcard of a house by the water on Lake Zurich. I have the crazy thought that I am entering a space that is occupied by Jung.

In a simple dinghy on the lake, a man is fishing. He is wearing a straw boater and has a pipe in his mouth. He turns and gives a little toss of his head, indicating that I am to join him. The next moment, I am in the boat, bobbing on the gentle waves of the lake. There are six silver fish around his feet. I remember that six was the number of the curious incidents involving fish that Jung wrote up as an example of how symbols can rhyme in a life.

There is nothing ghostly about the man in the boat. He is strong as a plowman. At first glance, he seems old, as he looks in later photographs. But his appearance shimmers. He shows himself as the virile young man who loved women, worked with Freud, and broke with him. He offers to show me his current home.

The boat skims us through the mist. A castle rises before us, with high stone walls, pointed rooftops, a tower that rises so high it vanishes in the mist.

"This is the Other Bollingen. It is the Bollingen I dreamed before I died. The reality of this place gave me the confidence to face death. I knew where I was going. Like you, I called it the Other Bollingen before I moved in. Now it is the true Bollingen, the Bollingen of the soul."

I feel all that the physical Bollingen meant to him. It was his sanctuary and his confession in stone. He worked stone with his own hands. He kept adding layers and levels, seeing a model of the psyche in his construction. We bump gently against a rock wall below a loggia. I follow Jung, thrilled with delight, from our landing place, across a forecourt with a huge carved stone, a perfect cube. I remember that in the ordinary world this stone had an extraordinary history.

"Yes, it is the stone the builders rejected."

This cube was delivered by mistake to the mason who was building a wall for Jung here. The mason, in a rage, wanted to send the stone back, but Jung, ever alert to how what humans see as accidents may be dice rolls by the gods, kept the cube and used it to memorialize his symbolic life. He carved the face of a Trickster, and words from Heraclitus; praise for Philemon, the spirit who walked with him in the garden; sympathy for a penitent Faust. As I recall, he left one of the faces of the cube blank. There is something there now, on this version. I lean forward to see the image, but Jung draws me away. Not yet. He has made many other changes.

We will converse in the tower. He has raised it toward the sky, high above the mists. I cannot estimate how many stories high. Ascending the spiral stair is effortless, a matter of floating rather than climbing. The walls are covered with cosmologies in brilliant colors.

Our conversation is uncertain, at the beginning. He knows my German is very poor, so he proposes that we talk in Latin. I confess that my Latin has been in full collapse for decades since I was given a prize in Latin class at school for drawing a picture of Julius Caesar standing before a map of Gaul. Jung's English is excellent, though heavily accented and not his preferred mode of discourse.

He shows me the book he has been writing in this Other Bollingen. Its cover is purple. Its title is *Liber Caelestis*. My Latin is sufficient to tell me that this is the Book of Heaven.

"This is my masterwork."

My hunger to know the contents is voracious. I have to restrain myself from trying to prize this masterwork from the master's hands.

I ask, "What is the most important thing you have discovered since you came here?"

"There is only one soul."

This both amazes and confounds me. Surely Jung, the great shaman-scholar of the West, has not veered into an Eastern vision of souls vanishing into a soup of golden light. His surroundings belie a belief in a nirvana that leaves behind the individual imagination and its prodigies.

"No, the individual is never erased. At the same time, the individual is a cell in the body of the Cosmic Being, of Adam Kadmon."

He speaks of the Teachers of the Deep, personified in archaic mythologies as amphibious beings — the Nommos of the Dogon, the Oannes of the Middle East, the dragon emperors of China — sometimes terrifying to look at.

"Those representations are true. It was these Teachers of the Deep that seeded intelligent life on Earth. They launched the experiment in consciousness that raised our kind from the primal swamp, to which we are forever seeking to return."

He speaks of lineages, of orders of initiates who communicate with each other across time and space and whose spirits are reborn within the orders.

"You and I belong to different lineages, similar but not the same. They, and we, have contended in certain lifetimes. We fought at Cyzicus. We came together to comprehend the mysteries of Ialdabaoth. We have parallel knowledge of a certain initiate who is dreaming our lives. When I lived on Earth, I saw him as a yogi. You have seen him as a Chaldean, wearing the bull horns."

We talk about his legacy. More than ever, he insists that he was never — and will never be — a Jungian. He disparages, gently, those who have turned his work into a catechism.

"My mind was always in motion. I was forever seeking new models of understanding, new words to explain ancient verities. Those who try to freeze my thought in static categories have no understanding of my mind or my character."

We talk about social life on the Other Side, and the current situation of people he knew in his earthly life.

"Freud is coming along. What he discovered on this side, when the veil fell from his eyes, was a profound shock to the old man. He had to become a child again, going to elementary school. But his love of literature and his willingness to trust to personal experience — and that dark Viennese humor — have helped him. We don't see much of each other, but I am happy to report that there are no bad feelings between us."

I am curious to know whether he is in touch with Mircea Eliade.

"I read the transcript of a conversation you had with Eliade that was published in a French magazine in the fifties. You used a phrase there that ignited my mind. Your dialogue moved to the phenomenon you called *synchronicity*. You said between flying parentheses that synchronicity is 'briefly, a rupture in time.' The phrase is burned deep in my memory. I hunted through your other writings, through your letters, through notes from your seminars, to see if you ever used that phrase again. It seemed that it vanished after that moment with Eliade, in whose style it was composed. I was disappointed, because it seemed to me that if you had written from that phrase, unfolding all that it contains, you would have given us a much better essay on synchronicity than the one you wrote."

"I do not disagree. But you can see that I have made my definitive rupture with time and can see all the patterns more clearly. And I have made my new book."

"Will we be able to read this? Will you hide it away, like *The Red Book*, or will you permit one or many to bring it through?"

"I am not looking for an amanuensis."

"And I have no wish to become one. I am asking whether you are willing to share some pages with those of us you are willing to receive. With your permission, I could invite a number of advanced students — dream archaeologists, shall we say — to come here, with me, as I invited them to travel to the Houses of Death, and beyond."

"That may be a bridge too far. But you have my permission to lead people into the dreams I recorded in my last life, and to introduce them to my essential practices. On that front, I want to give you more. Exercises and techniques that I have developed since I left the body. There are themes involved that are essential for your world, even for the survival of humanity. I will give you ways of understanding and coping with the egregores, the collective thought-forms. And with mythic irruptions, when the raw power of an archetype floods the tiny dry creek bed of the ordinary mind. We must discuss building psychic cages to contain the toxic entities that again threaten to possess the minds of whole nations."

Jung indicates that this is enough for one visit.

I am curious to know about his personal life. There is no sign of a companion on the levels of the house that he opened to me. Is he no longer in contact with either of his two wives, Emma and Toni Wolff?

"They are walking on other paths now."

He confides, with the shyness of a boy, that he has a new partner, an English beauty. He will not introduce us, at least not yet. But I realize that her presence in his astral sanctuary may have increased his willingness to talk with me in the English language.

He escorts me down to the courtyard. I am still eager to see what is carved now on the face of the cube that was formerly blank.

I am pulled away, as if by an invisible wind dragon.

"Dream on it. Dreams are the facts from which we must proceed."

2

In his life on Earth, Jung understood very well that we can talk to the dead. Like his mother, he constantly felt himself in the presence of the departed. He recorded dreams in which the deceased came to him for instruction. He floated the idea that the souls of the dead "know only what they knew at the moment of death, and nothing beyond that. Hence their endeavor to penetrate into life in order to share in the knowledge of man. I frequently have a feeling that they are standing directly behind us, waiting to hear what answer we will give to them, and what answer to destiny."

It is clear that his opinion has evolved.

Dreams and visions set us research assignments, and this was the pattern of Jung's life. As he neared physical death, he made this statement: "All day long I have exciting ideas and thoughts. But I take up in my work only those to which my dreams direct me."

In the spirit of Jung, I accepted that our conversation — which took place while I was drumming for a group shamanic journey on a mountain in Transylvania — had given me leads that demanded some dream archaeology, which of necessity must be both scholarly and experiential. There were those rare names to be traced. There was the provocative suggestion that Jung might have things to teach us about how to confront the dark forces of the collective Shadow in our own time. Above all, it was eminently desirable to return to the Other Bollingen and see whether the sage of the lake might reveal more of his Purple Book, or the sources from which it sprang.

The barbarous name Ialdabaoth comes from Gnostic theology, which appealed to Jung more than it appeals to me. It takes us into the realm of demiurges and that old rooster god Abraxas, which colored Jung's *Seven Sermons to the Dead* and runs as a deep underground river — sometimes bursting through to the surface — in his depth psychology.

Cyzicus struck a distant chord. The ancient town stood on the coast of Mysia, in what is now northwestern Turkey. Many battles were fought there in recorded history, including a great sea battle in 410 BC, when an Athenian fleet destroyed the Spartans. There is a stranger and older battle in the mythic story of the Golden Fleece. King Cyzicus — the town took its name from him — gave hospitality to Jason and the Argonauts. But when the voyagers were blown back to the city in a night storm, the town's defenders thought they were enemies, and in the bloody melee that followed, the king was killed. The chaos was said to have been caused by the anger of the Great Goddess of Anatolia, named in this version as Cybele.

I felt the recognition that comes with goosebumps. I knew a little of what it means to incur the wrath of that goddess. I still bear the mark over my left kidney.

At home on a frigid day at the turn of the year, with taps left dripping through the house in hopes of preventing the pipes from freezing, I mined the best of all research sources for a dream archaeologist: my journal from forty years. Many handwritten notebooks still await transcription, which may never come about, since my writing is mostly indecipherable even to me. But a search of my data files in Word pulled up a reference to Cyzicus in a journal entry from more than twenty years before. I had actually titled the report "Dream Archaeology: The Keys to Mantis."

In the dream, I studied relief carvings from an ancient site called Mantis, which means *prophet* or *seer*. My dream self — often much wiser than me — had found a way to bring together fragments that previous scholars had been unable to connect. When the pattern emerged, it gave the key to an ancient mystery encoded in an epic poem called the *Arimaspea*.

This was my dream. My research at the time revealed that the *Arimaspea* is known to history only from a passage in Herodotus that contains a wild story of a shaman poet named Aristeas who died and came back, could leave his body at will, and was known to appear in two places at once. He entered a workshop where fullers were cleaning wool on his home island on the Sea of Marmara and promptly fell down dead. The people from the shop closed their doors and ran to get his family. They encountered a man who had just arrived by boat from Cyzicus. He told them that Aristeas was alive and well; he had just seen him over there. Everyone rushed back to the fuller's shop and found no sign of a body, dead or alive.

Aristeas vanished for a few years, then returned from adventures among a mysterious mountain people, the Arimaspi, who fought with griffins over gold. This was the theme of his lost epic. The shaman poet turned up again at a Greek colony in Italy two centuries later. The locals were greatly impressed by his powers and saw him as a possible avatar, and certainly a favorite, of Apollo, to whom they erected a new temple. Aristeas now revealed that his soul left his body through his mouth in the form of a raven, the sacred bird of Apollo.

This was thrilling stuff, though it did not answer the question of who was who in an ancient battle at Cyzicus.

I wrenched myself away from journal mining and book searches to focus on the most pressing question: was Jung willing to release more from the Purple Book and, above all, to offer us some counsel in our distressing times? This was, after all, the man who had analyzed Hitler, had premonitory visions of two world wars, and cautioned about how much in the world can go wrong when a man possessed by the wrong archetype rises to power on its dark wings and possesses the mind of a whole collective.

Channeling was one option. But I'm not given either to automatic writing or to dictation from a trance state, though it runs in the family. My great-aunt, the opera singer, foresaw my death when I was three years old. She was correct. However, she did not see that I was going to come back.

I decided to attempt another journey to the Other Bollingen in the same way my unexpected visit had begun: by using shamanic drumming to travel into the imaginal realm. I invited two veteran dream travelers to come with me, forming a dream-archaeology team. They were both young, lively, attractive women, and I thought they might appeal to Jung. They were both athletic. One loved water sports, the other martial arts and capoeira. I will call them the Mermaid and the Kickboxer.

We needed to agree on our shared mission. We decided it was to seek permission to bring back ideas and information from the book Jung has written on the Other Side. The starting point for the girls would be Jung himself, on the boat. Since I had already been to the Other Bollingen, I felt I could simply turn up at the door. It was understood that, while we would try to keep track of each other during the journey, our primary assignment was to try to get information by whatever methods worked.

Before we started, the Kickboxer became quite emotional. The after-death locale had made her think of her brother, who had died very young. She apologized that she might not be able to keep her focus on the group mission. I took her hand and told her that it was enough to do her best, and let her feelings power her understanding that we can have helpful encounters with the departed on their own ground.

While I beat the drum, and kept an eye on the group, a vital part of my consciousness flew straight to Jung's tower on the lake. I was met at the door by a man I had never seen before. Blocky, stubby, his shoulders barely fitting his dress jacket, he looked like a bodyguard posing as a butler. I knew his name was Hermann. I was not happy to see him, and he was certainly not happy to see me.

"Herr Doktor Jung is not available," he snapped. "And you do not have his permission to invite other guests to the main house."

However, Hermann did not slam the door. He informed me that a room had been prepared where they could view certain images and a few pages from the book. It had also been arranged for the Kickboxer to meet her brother.

She turned up quite promptly. I did not yet know how she had gained Jung's permission, or if she had succeeded in getting into the boat with him. I shadowed her to a room where I saw a drawing I did not understand. It might have been the flayed skin of an animal hanging from a rack, or wrinkled sheets, or falling water.

Pages of what I assumed was the Purple Book were laid out on a table. I saw the Mermaid come in. She kept looking over her shoulder. Following her gaze, I saw the Kabbalistic Tree of Life, rising level upon level.

I went looking for Jung. I found him walking a path in the woods, arm in arm with a lovely young woman with light-brown hair in a light-yellow dress. When Jung turned to me, I was not introduced. He was clearly irritated, and perhaps surprised, that I had found him in this private area. Still, he was gracious. He allowed me to look over the contents page of his Book of Heaven. He made it clear that deeper knowledge would have to be earned by following these leads.

In a warming mood, Jung told me he could arrange for me to be welcomed by more of the Jungian groups and to speak to them. "However, there are some of them who won't forgive you for saying that you are in direct contact with me, *especially if they believe this is true.*"

We had done enough. I sounded the recall on my drum. After a few minutes of quiet time to make notes and recover, we shared our travel reports. The Kickboxer said, "I went straight to the boat and approached Jung as a mermaid. This got his attention. On the lake wall I met my brother, the one who died so young" — her eyes were shining — "and he was with me for the rest of the journey. We entered a room where some pages of a book were laid out on a table. There was a drawing of a waterfall that became a portal. I fell at amazing speed, down and down, over many cascades until I found myself in a circle of the dead who are living here."

The Mermaid said, "I went to the boat too. I became a little yellow bird on Jung's shoulder. I stayed with him, in bird form, as he returned to his house. When he reached the door, I appeared in human form in a light-yellow dress, taking care to make myself as charming and beautiful as possible. He responded very well. He took me up in the tower. The paintings seemed to be a continuous Tree of Life, predominantly rendered in gold. There was the sense that ascending was descending, that the way up is also the way down."

There was more. She drew diagrams and symbols she was shown in the special display room. The central feature of one was a six-pointed star. Another, lozenge-shaped, represented a complex mirror effect, generating parallel realities.

They turned to me for my own report. I had already lost some of the chapter titles of the Purple Book, but not the title Jung has chosen for the introduction to his masterwork:

Why I Am Not a Jungian

Dream Interruptus

How many lives are you living right now? That's a bear of a question.

"Why aren't you in bed with me?"

I was shocked to see Amanda getting dressed. I looked at the beautiful slopes of her body, the perfect globes of her breasts. I had longed for her across the years of our separation. I jumped from under the covers and nuzzled her neck, touching the places where she had always been most easily aroused. She moved away, breaking contact in a way that was painful, because I was hard and urgent to be inside her.

"Don't tell me you don't remember." Her luscious red lips tightened into a straight line.

"It was beautiful," I said uncertainly, trying to remember what was going on earlier. I remembered the thrill of sneaking into this apartment like naughty high-school seniors. The apartment belonged to a friend who was away. I knew that he never locked the windows at the back, so we had left the car down the street, scampered through the garden, and climbed into the guest room at the back. We were now in the master bedroom, because there was plenty of room to romp on that king-size bed.

And we had been romping royally, hadn't we? I was ready to explode as soon as she took off her blouse, and I knew when I touched her between her legs that she was more than ready for me. Years of age and of absence fell away. She was as beautiful and as sexy as she had been on our first date at the fish restaurant, when she wore a pink dress and swallowed two plates of oysters and said — when we were on the second bottle of bubbly — "I think really good friends should make love together, don't you?"

I sat back down on the bed, with my face in my hands, trying to remember what had happened to make her so mad at me. We had finished tearing off each other's clothes — then we were all over each other, on the bed — and I was about to penetrate her — and...

I did not know what happened next, except that we did not have sex. It wasn't a failed performance. Had I blacked out? We hadn't been drinking, and I didn't use any other kind of drugs. Had I fallen asleep? How was that possible, with so much energy raging in me and between us?

I was called away.

It suddenly hit me. One moment I was on the bed with her, hungry for sex after long starvation. The next moment I was somewhere else. Where, why, how?

I am suddenly there, in the place I must have been when I went missing from the love bed. I am lumbering like a bear walking on two legs. No, that's not quite right. I *am* a bear, walking like a man. I have an assignment. There is someone in urgent need of healing and protection, someone who needs me *now*. She is very young and very frightened, and there is no way I am going to let her down.

In my great hairy body I am crossing a chaotic hospital lobby.

Nobody seems to notice that a bear has walked in. I ride the elevator up to a high floor. I hesitate in the corridor. Then I see her, the girl who needs me. "Mister Bear!" she beams. She hugs the bear the way she hugs her teddy. "I knew you were coming."

I take her by the hand and sit her down on a sofa in a waiting area near the restrooms. "I want you to stay right here," I told her. "Don't talk to strangers and don't go wandering off, okay?"

"Can't I go get a snack?"

"Not till later, sweetie. Wait till I come get you. Then Nana will take you."

I leave Ellie on the sofa, swinging her legs. I walk down the hall in the direction she came from. I ignore the red light above the door of the operating room. The door opens, and I am among doctors and nurses in scrubs and breathing masks. They have opened Ellie's body, the one she left in here when she went walking down the hall. Nobody pays any attention to the bear in the room.

I scan the space. They can see me, and some try to hide, slithering behind medical equipment, diving under the bed, crowding into a darker corner up under the ceiling. One tries to lie flat against a drip line, pretending he is part of the setup. I make that little coughing sound in the chest that bears make when they start to get mad. Some of the *sluagh* — the restless dead; the old Irish name fits them well — flit out of the room. But some are still hovering, hungering, waiting for their chance.

It's mine, one of them hisses. *I got here first.*

The thing shows itself as it was — a disgusting, toothless old man with sagging dewlaps. It leans over the body on the operating table. It hoists a leg. It's trying to climb into the girl's body.

I take him out. The blow from the bear's giant paw scatters the hungry ghost like a mess of chicken bones.

There is no reasoning with hospital spooks of this type. I've had to deal with them many times. The problem with hospitals is not that so many people die in them, but that lots of them don't leave when they die. They've had no preparation for what comes after the death of the body, or they have forgotten, so they hover around the last place where they were alive. Sometimes they don't even get out of the intensive-care unit or shared ward where they died. They drift around in sick, diseased shadow forms, their butts hanging out of their hospital gowns. Then sometimes they get a whiff of fresh meat — a body still healthy enough to make home if they can manage to move in. That's when the body snatching, or attempted home invasion, begins.

General anesthesia is meant to drive soul — even if doctors won't call it that — out of the body. That creates an opportunity for unauthorized entry by another soul, one of those hungry ghosts. This is why you don't want to let yourself be knocked out by anesthesia in hospital unless there is someone to watch over you.

That is why I am here, loaded as bear. To watch over Ellie, my best friend's little girl, who has been like a daughter to me.

The atmosphere in the operating room has been transformed. It is filling with friendly spirits. Can that be Ellie's grandfather?

I watch the medical team remove the appendix, stitch the girl's body up, rinse off. They look at clocks. They discuss how long it will be before she wakes up as they wheel her into recovery. Time to go find the Ellie I left on the couch by the elevators.

"I was very good, Mister Bear," she greets me. "Do I get a treat now?"

"We'll have a teddy-bear picnic later on," I promise. I take her hand and lead her to recovery. We swing our arms and sing,

Today's the day the teddy bears have their picnic

At the bedside, I pass my hand over Ellie's eyes. Unlike the Men in Black, I don't have a neuralyzer to erase memories. A simple pass is enough. All I want to do is to blur the transition, so Ellie will wake in her body with just a lovely dream about a bear.

"That bed looks so comfy," I suggest. "Why don't you lie down and take a little nap? I'll tuck you up nice and tight."

She smiles and yawns and slips into her body as easily as she might have pulled up the sheets.

Amanda was putting on her power boots, the ones with four-inch heels. She said, "I'm leaving first. By the front door, like a grown-up. Give me five minutes' start."

Her eyes dropped. She could see I was still standing like a flagstaff.

"I don't know how you could just check out with that part of you so — upstanding. Must be the booze."

She brushed my lips with her mouth.

"It was really good before, wasn't it?" I instantly regret saying that.

"You are the love of my life," she said. I couldn't see this in her eyes, because she had put on the oversized Sophia Loren sunglasses I detested.

"Just not in this life."

"Not when you can't stay with me where we are."

I don't recall the rest of the conversation. I'm not even sure that she left the apartment. I seem to remember us back on a bed, but a different bed — a single bed, the kind you can push together with another, which in this case was on the other side of a little table. I wanted her urgently, and although she was still mad and sad and holding back, I could feel her body eager to receive me.

Then grinding of a different kind called me away. I opened my eyes and realized I was at home in my usual bed and that the sound was the noise of my current girlfriend grinding coffee beans for the first caffeine infusion of the day.

I pulled on my robe, rinsed my mouth with Fresh Burst, and padded down the hall to the kitchen.

"I see you made it through the night," said Vivien, handing me a mug.

I did not tell her I'd been with another woman, or that the scene with Amanda was as real to me as — maybe more real than — the scene in the kitchen. I turned on the TV in the living room. The national nightmare was still playing, each installment crazier than the last. I had promised myself that one day I would wake up and find, along with everyone else, that we had left this alternate reality and returned to a sane world. Not yet.

I could not shake the feeling that my unconsummated tryst with Amanda was quite real, that we had been together in our physical bodies. Could what I would now describe as a dream be a scene from a continuous life that Amanda and I were living in a parallel world that was different from the one I was in, sipping my coffee in front of TV?

It was tantalizing that the dream interruptus was so close to my present event track. Amanda and I had broken up, painfully, years before, as in the dream. I had dreamed of a life in which we had stayed together, and that life had not seemed happy at all. This was a further variant.

I had been so excited in that bedroom. Yet I had been called from lovemaking by something stronger, the need to be present for a child who was at risk of things I couldn't easily explain to the people who were at the hospital with her.

How many lives was I living right now? Which of the dreams was most real?

The phone rang. My friend told me, "I thought you'd want to know that Ellie did fine. She wants to tell you something."

When she came on the phone, Ellie spoke in a conspiratorial hush. "You'll never guess what happened. *Mister Bear* came to see me in the hospital."

World War I Will End in 2018

You stand at the center of all times. There are places where it is easier to remember this, and to act on it. The Gallery of Time is one of them. It is a real place in the imaginal realm.

"Today we are going to the Gallery of Time," I explain to the eager group of adventurers gathered in a restored stone farmhouse in the Midi.

"This is a place where many have gone to explore their connections with personalities living in other times. It will appear to you like a very long, well-lit gallery filled with art and artifacts, furniture and clothing, jewelry and masks and weapons from many different cultures. You will be drawn to one of these. When you look at that picture, or try on that coat, or sit on that chaise longue, you will be instantly drawn into the time and place from which it comes. You will find yourself entering the experiences of someone who belongs to that time. You may feel yourself entering the mind of this person and settling into his or her body for a while.

"You need to clarify all the details. Whose life have you entered? What exactly is going on?

"You want to establish why you have been drawn to this person. How do the dramas and issues of this life situation compare to your own? Are there lessons to be drawn?

"Remember that the time is now. You may be able to establish clear mental communication with the personality whose situation you have entered. You can initiate mental dialogue. You may find that there are ways in which you can help each other, at least to understand a transtemporal drama."

I had already introduced them to the Gatekeeper and given them a password. You don't get to the Gallery of Time — let alone what lies beyond it — without an invitation and certain preparation. I am eager to see what today's travelers, all bright and eager and ready, would bring back from this new expedition to a place where I have conducted hundreds of voyagers over the years.

"Put your bodies into correct position for the journey," I remind them. Soon they are stretched out comfortably on the mats, eyes covered by sleep shades or bandannas.

I drum for the group, and travel with them. While watching over the group, both physically and psychically, I am ready to make a personal journey. I have a low boredom threshold and have learned that the mind can be fully active in several places — levels of consciousness *and* reality — at once.

I watch our travelers salute the Gatekeeper, who takes forms adjusted to their own characters and experience.

I am detained in my own journey by unexpected activity around the steps to the great building. An old friend, who handles security here, appears dressed like a gamekeeper, in tweeds, with a shotgun over his arm. Men in similar garb, and some in British military uniforms of perhaps a century ago, are coming and going and keeping close watch on the perimeter. My friend is welcoming, and approving of my guests. But he wants me to understand that there is something urgent I must do, something to do with the military.

I enter the gallery and realize I am in a military section, with uniforms, helmets, and weapons on display. My attention is captured by an officer's Sam Browne belt — combining a shoulder belt and a regular belt, with a leather holster attached, and a heavy pistol inside.

I strap these on.

Immediately I join the situation of a young British officer in the trenches in the thick of World War I. His first name is Norman. He has not been having a good war. His commanding officer — not a bad fellow, Norman is eager to explain — considered him a coward for holding back when ordered to take his men out of shelter into the German machine-gun fire. The colonel died doing just that.

The year is 1916. This world of mud and blood is part of the Battle of the Somme.

Norman can't breathe. He is buried under a heap of dead and dying men. No one is coming to help. He is going to die like this, breath forced from his lungs.

What he most wants now is a glimpse of blue sky and green hills.

In my mind, I am driving on a curving road, over gently rolling hills. In part of myself, I am back in upstate New York circa 1987, on a road I often drove while living on a farm near Chatham. I am drinking the fresh air through the open window, delighting in the sweet beauty of the green rolling hills, the horses grazing, the glorious blue sky with a few fluffy fair-weather clouds, all more vivid than I had previously remembered.

"Thank you," Norman groans. I am amazed to realize that,

without knowing what I was doing, I have placed happy memories from my life in upstate New York a quarter century ago into the mind of a man who is dying in a trench in Europe in 1916.

"I want to give you something," Norman speaks in my mind. "I was good at drawing. I was a fair draftsman. I helped design an engine. That may be old hat to you, I know, but please use anything I can give."

Now I understand the military theme at the entrance to the Gallery of Time. I did not come here today to fulfill an agenda set by my current self, but to answer a call from almost a century ago. I am moved to tears by the thought that I may have been called, in this simple way, to give a dying soldier a glimpse of blue sky.

We stand at the center of all times.

There are places where it is easier to remember this, and to act on it. The Gallery of Time is one of them.

When we come across something as important as this, the world often helps us to hold on to it by producing a rhyme.

The day after I entered the mind of a dying man in World War I, I ran into a man who had taken part in my workshop, while waiting for a flight to Paris at Montpellier airport. He is from Sweden, and had proved himself to be an excellent travel companion in more than one reality over the three days of our adventure.

I described my visit to the dying man in World War I.

My Swedish friend said, "World War I will end in 2018."

"I beg your pardon?"

He repeated, "World War I will end in 2018." He explained that this line is part of the promo for a TV series on World War I that was running in Sweden.

The Emperor
of Enchantment

The imaginal realm has countless architects. Every dream traveler who goes there contributes to its design. Some of the most alluring constructs are devised by the Emperor of Enchantment and his army of industrious djinns. Lost boys and lost girls who left the ordinary world when it was too lonely or too mean migrate here, like Peter Pan. If you follow their trail, you may be able to bring home your own magical child. But step carefully in the lands of enchantment. It may be easier to get in than to get out.

I've been meeting again with the Emperor of Enchantment in a certain quarter of the imaginal realm, somewhere beyond the swamp of half-forgotten dreams, but a far journey from the scholar city of Anamnesis. He shows himself without ostentation, in a smoke-colored burnoose like a man of the desert, sometimes riding a mighty smoke-colored horse.

I first met him in a busy open-air market alive with flashing colors and the rich aromas of cardamom, coffee, and jasmine. I

was drawn at first, naturally, to the alley of the old-book dealers. The billowing white canopies above their stalls recalled my
boyhood sessions reading under the sheets with a flashlight after
my mother had issued firm instructions to go to sleep. I thought
I might find a rare volume that has long eluded me, a chronicle
from an eastern kingdom, known to Marco Polo, that is said to
contain the true story of the Magi. That book eluded me still, but
I was delighted to rediscover a companion of my youth, a tale in
which the hero can only get to the object of his desire by enchant-
ing the guardians of a magic apple orchard by making up stories.

I walked on, down the alley of the bird sellers. The best of
them had no need for cages. They displayed their birds on flower-
ing golden bushes from which the birds had no desire to fly away
until the right person appeared.

I came to a humble section of the market. The stalls seemed
to be devoted to items rescued from attics and garages — broken
toys and disheveled dolls. Nonetheless, I was drawn to a stand
where the dealer had spread his wares on a rug on the ground.
There was something familiar about a knight in armor whose
horse was missing one leg. He was the old kind of lead soldier you
don't find anymore; now they make toy soldiers out of pewter or
plastic. A scene hovered before me like a mirage floating out of a
heat haze, of a set of these knights, both mounted and on foot, on
a tray table over a hospital bed, where a sick boy was too weak to
avoid spilling them, one by one, to break on the floor.

I squatted down to inspect the lead knight more closely. Then
he appeared, cloaked to the eyes in his smoke-colored garment.
His black eyes glowed like coals. He smelled of cumin, smoked
meat, and the absence of oranges. His presence was eerie and un-
settling, but fascinating. He indicated that I should inspect the
contents of the stall very carefully. I could take any item I chose,

but I should choose wisely, because each item opened a different door.

I studied a little pair of opera glasses wrapped in mother-of-pearl, a hand-me-down from my great-aunt, the opera singer. I remembered using these glasses at a matinee when I was possibly ten years old to get a better look at the pretty girl leading the Mickey Mouse Club songs. There were many things. A teddy bear, a strange ring, a cardboard periscope, a miniature chess set, a spaceman's gun.

I picked up the knight whose horse had a broken leg. Instantly I heard the stirring and snorting and stamping of great horses. Beyond the market, beyond a high wall I had not noticed until now, was some kind of stable. There was no gate in the wall, but as I hurried toward it, with my boyhood toy in my hand, the wall opened, and a great horse with a star on its forehead trotted out to meet me.

This was the start of my adventures in the Empire of Enchantment. There is something you should know about it right now. It is easier to get in than to get out. That is why some parts of you — a lost girl or a lost boy or a lost traveler among the Mountains of the Moon — may be living there, gone from you for longer than you remembered until now.

Exploring Old Town

We dream travelers make our own maps. We may start by using directions and tips from previous voyagers, even ancient charts. But we go beyond all of these into terra incognita. As we journey, we not only make roads where there were none before; we shape cities and mountain ranges. These can then be visited by other travelers. Each new visit will help make our created realities stronger and more durable.

There is an Old Town in the Real City. How can a city be real without one?

I climbed the Spindle in the Plaza Mayor to get the general layout. The stone giants that guard the Spindle sprang up at my approach, hackles raised, but relaxed when they smelled cinnamon. From the observation module, five hundred feet up, the roofs of Old Town rise and fall like a choppy umber sea within its ancient walls. There is no impression of central planning here. Nothing runs straight in Old Town. The number of its hills is disputed. To the northeast, below the walls, they fall to the bank of Deep River.

Descending from the Spindle, I took the diagonal street that runs back from the corner of the plaza between City Hall and the Real Museum to the Gate of Intention in the Old Town wall. I found the gate closed, and the gatekeeper took his sweet time before pulling back the shutter behind the barred window in the side door. I saw only his nose and chin inside the hood, as he stood in three-quarter profile. He wanted a name, and it seemed my ordinary name would not do.

I was inspired to say "Cuthbert." I have no idea why. The gatekeeper grunted, and I remembered the token. I took it from my pocket. It looked like a coin from an antique currency, golden in color but too light to be actual gold. I put it in the slot beside the gate. The machine spat it out. I caught it before it fell to the ground, recalling the most important bit: the token must be charged with intention and carry a valid character imprint. Not everyone is up to charging a token for Old Town, and many have faulty character codes, but some such may gain entry at this gate if they come with a token prescription from the Genealogy Office at the Healing Center.

I held the token between my thumb and my third finger and willed my intention into the coin. When its center was warm and amber-bright, I dropped it in the slot.

Immediately I heard creaking and groaning, not only in the hinges of the great gate, but in the Old Town behind the walls. I understood — if only obscurely — that when the charge of an intention is received, the Old Town transforms.

I stepped through the gateway into a narrow, twisting alley, barely wide enough for my broad shoulders to pass without my having to walk sideways. The statue of a knight in armor greeted me with a leering wink and held out a wineskin. Not right now. I would need my senses keenly alert to get through the Street of the Drunken Knight without crashing into one of the doors that kept opening and closing, offering distractions and temptations.

I made it through the narrow passage. Ahead was a bridge over a canal, lined with houses in the Dutch style. I recognized the tallest of the houses on my left. I had been here before, coming a different way. Inside, I had found the armaments of an old-time magus, including a flying carpet and a complicated but service-able apparatus that looked like a cross between an espresso ma-chine and a 3D model of the Kabbalistic Tree of Life. No time to linger here now, but I marked the location for a future visit.

I looked down into the dark water of the canal and recoiled. On its blurry currents bobbed things people had dropped and forgotten. It was a place of memory loss, not release. On the right side of the bridge, an animal came running. Could it be a weasel? I named this crossing the Bridge of the Weasel. A tricky name, with vicious teeth. Yet to name something is to anchor it in its world. The bridge now seemed very strong, a route to be counted on.

On the far side, I saw a house with the gilded head of a re-triever above the door. The House of the Golden Dog. Interesting, but I did not enter, merely noting the address for a future visit. The street now divided. I took the right-hand branch and soon came into an irregular cobbled square, and knew at once that I had reached the Place of High Magic.

Another breathing statue, wings outspread, rose from a col-umn in the center. When I moved my eyes from it, the angel — or daimon — floated high into the air, returning to its imperson-ation of a stationary being when I returned my gaze. When I shifted my attention to the many-storied building to the right, the winged figure was there before me, now sporting the feathered cap and sandals of Mercury. This building, again, was familiar. I stepped through the doors into the Tarot Café. The fug of tobacco smoke was as heavy as I remembered. The larger-than-life forms of the Greater Trumps glowered or beamed, forever revolving, in the images on the walls. A ruddy-faced, grinning barkeep pressed a pot of wheat beer, spiked with raspberry syrup, into my hand, and I raised it in a toast. A scholar in rimless glasses invited me to travel with him across the desert of Daath on the path of the High Priestess. Maybe later. A woman with white-blond hair, wearing a black eye patch, offered me the Lovers card. Not here, not now.

Near the Mercury building I found the Lapis Lounge, where alchemists still debate the principles of Nicolas Flamel and pursue his quest for the philosophers' stone. On the left side of the square was Finn's Fishhouse, under the sign of a bronze salmon and a hazel tree. The specialty of the house, of course, is planked salmon, served with a hazel wand and filberts, in memory of the great fish that ate of the tree of wisdom that stood beside the River Boyne, and gave the gifts of seership to the first Irish shaman.

I had no time to look further around the Place of High Magic. I hurried down steep flights of steps to the Place of Low Magic. It was a melee of fire-eaters, gypsy fortune tellers, vendors of charms and relics, greasy palm readers, and bloated mediums. A busker with a black bird on his shoulder invited me to step inside a tent where my most intimate problems would be solved by a talking head, one clipped from Great Bran, no less.

I stepped on briskly, climbing a shorter flight of stone steps, and found myself at a lively pub under the sign of The Cock & Bull. This was irresistible. I crossed the threshold, into a pleasant swill of words, warm and spicy as mulled wine. No habitué of this establishment was less than a wordslinger worthy to sit at table with Kit Marlowe or Dylan Thomas or the Great Bard himself. They flowered and flourished in iambic pentameters and countless meters unpenned. To breathe the air in the saloon bar was to come away high with English as few English have ever spoken it.

I walked on, through a street market where the barrows and shop windows were filled to bursting with good things, from old books and birds of paradise to ripe figs and cheeses and wines.

The market ended at a pleasant green, beyond which rose a square pink house, again familiar from some other travels, whether through the Gates of Day or the Gates of Night I cannot say. As I entered, a dimpled maid helped me to shrug off the cloak I had not known I was wearing until now. As I handed her my silver-topped stick, I knew I had arrived at the Pink House of Madame Beth.

Everyone was dressed to the nines, in the style of long ago. Most of the gentlemen wore white-tie and tails, the ladies long dresses with plunging décolletages. Woe befall any who think of Madame Beth's as a mere bordello. This is a most select establishment, a *maison de rendezvous* where partners may be highly practiced, but are not professionals. I observed some courtship dances, and considered some willing partners among the ladies, but was not permitted to stray for long from my mission in the Old Town.

I left Madame Beth's discreetly, by the side entrance and a door in the garden wall, and headed down to the river. It was now long past curfew, but I knew that the Watch would not oppose a traveler going in this direction. Below the eastern wall of Old Town, where the hills drop sharply to the river bank, is a kind of *terrain vague*. I sat at the fado café and listened to the keening of a fiddle and then to an achingly beautiful female voice that opened my tear ducts. A solemn waiter brought me a plate of linguiça and a glass of dry white port, which I sipped as the musical assassin stabbed my heart with her exquisite song of a lost country and a lost love.

I watched the cabin lights of a motor launch on the river. I was tempted to join one of these night cruises, but I knew it would end where Real City ends, at an invisible barrier that turns you around until, without intending it, you are headed back to where you came from.

The Fifty-Ninth Swan

In a lovely, slender book of memories and verse, *Some Memories of W. B. Yeats*, the English poet John Masefield describes his visit to the Irish poet and magus in his rooms off Tavistock Square in London in 1900. "That curved stair, lit by a little lamp at the curve, was trodden by all who made our world." There is a poem that compares Yeats to Finn, an ancient high king of Ireland, playing a kind of Celtic chess with human-sized knights on a board big enough for hurling. The king suggests to them that if they use their minds properly, they can bring the game pieces to life. This is possible, he explains, if we raise a condition of "high excitement."

Suppose we could fold time and visit young Willie Yeats at the top of that curved stair, as he seeks to raise "high excitement" as he wages a magical battle with the "Great Beast" Aleister Crowley and pursues the woman he loves with fierce but unrequited passion...

1

The poet shakes his long head when he laughs, then throws it back so his mane of dark hair flies off his forehead. His long artist's fingers make brushstrokes in the air.

He pauses when Mrs. Old, who is both his landlady and his cook, returns to clear the dishes from their simple dinner — beef stew, apple pie, and a decent burgundy. Mrs. Old is proud of her tenant and delights in fussing over him. Such a grand gentleman, she says, who lends a bit of quality to the neighborhood, and doesn't talk like an Irishman at all. "The toff in the Woburn Buildings," the shopkeeper next door calls Mr. Yeats. Mrs. Old considers the guests who come up the curved stair to his sitting room for his Monday evenings "at home" to be quality too. Some come in evening dress, others in velvet or country tweeds. Some of the poet's women — and there are almost as many as he has books on his crowded shelves — are flashy, but in the style of great ladies of the stage, not of the music hall.

While Mrs. Old removes the tablecloth, the poet goes to the window and looks down at the court. The lamplight throws shadows from the plane trees onto the tired row houses across the street, restoring their looks and adding a touch of mystery. The blind man is still at his post under the lamp, swaying from foot to foot, offering matches and shoelaces on a little wooden tray to late walkers coming home from the pubs or the station.

Yeats pulls the heavy blue drapes closed and places the red clay jar on the table. It has the raised design of a pair of black dragons. The magic, for now, is only Virginia tobacco. As a blue haze rises in the air, there is a rattle in his throat that turns into a nasty liquid cough.

"I would smoke less if I were you, Willie. We must not lose your glorious voice." Isabella Augusta Gregory, now removing her shawl, is the first of his guests tonight. She only calls him Willie in private. He always calls her Lady Gregory. It sets a boundary, which they both know to be essential; she has devoted her life to him since her husband died.

The other guests come up the curved stair in ones and twos. There cannot be many; the room is of modest size, even when the table is moved to the side. There is the lovely actress Florence Farr, his sister in the Order, who has stood side by side with him through the magical battles and diabolical attacks that have depleted him and made him sick and paler than ever. There is Dorothea, another of the beautiful women he might have had — if he could permit himself to have any woman except the one who will not have him — and her earnest, admiring husband from Galway. W. T. Stead is an unexpected but very welcome guest. He is a crusading journalist for causes of which Yeats and his women mostly approve (though Maud does not like many English causes), such as the rescue of child prostitutes. Above all, Stead is a relentless and fervent investigator of psychic phenomena, and Yeats has become a regular at the séances he hosts at his rambling home in Wimbledon.

Last to arrive are the American Van Meter and his lady friend, who claims an Italian title but talks in the accent of New Jersey. Van Meter has money and owns a publishing house. His money would not normally buy him entry to the poet's salon, even though Yeats has precious little of it, but Van Meter has been buying pictures from Yeats's profligate father in New York.

The poet's guests expect him to read poetry to them, and he does. If they are disappointed that he does not have new work to share, or that his voice is less thrilling than it has seemed to them on other evenings, they mask their feelings. He is a poet who has not been writing poetry for almost two years. He has gone on cranking out articles and reviews — writers must *write* — but these are no substitute.

He knows why the sacred spring ceased to flow. He can never

forget the day Maud stood with the sunrise in her hair and asked him what he had dreamed. He told her with honesty, though he turned down his head in shyness, that he had dreamed of kissing her. "Then kiss me now," she said. He kissed her, awkwardly, a clumsy boy. But she smiled on him with loving eyes and told him that in *her* dream, that same night, they had been summoned by a god and married under the shining Spear of Lugh.

The dream was magnificent. It held the promise — no, more than that, the actual fulfillment — of everything he had yearned for and asked for since, seven years before, he first set eyes on a woman more beautiful than any he had seen or imagined. He had written the best of his poetry for her, giving her the names of high queens and goddesses. He had begged her, again and again, to marry him. But on that early December day in 1898, when Maud stood with her dream trailing its glory all about her, and reached to him with her lovely white arms, her lips swelling red with passion...he did not rise. He fled. He did not run from the room at once, but he fled within. He fled from the sudden heat of her body, the swell of her breast, the flush rising to the root of her throat.

He withdrew deeper inward when she bared her secret life and told him that for all the time she had known him, she had been sleeping with another man — a violent *married* man to whom she had borne children. This man was neither Irish nor English, but a French politician deep in a world of spies and conspiracies. Yeats must have known something of this, in the part of him that was an instinctive man, and the part that dreamed in the night. Maud told him she had broken with Millevoye, again offering the poet his opportunity to seize and manifest the dream. But her confession threw him into deeper confusion and darkened his sight. Now he noticed the little spray of lines at the edges of her eyes, the thickening of the waist that might go with motherhood. She was no longer the most beautiful woman in the world. Still less was she the faery bride, the woman without a shadow, that he had insisted the poet in him needed more than any woman of sex and skin. All of this cut him so deeply that his soul climbed to a stone keep on a high lonely place, where bones creak in the wind and human-headed birds flap over gray bogs and barrens.

He spoke wan words to her, of how they were destined to have a "spiritual marriage" and not an embodied one, holding to the theory that the poet in his soul could flourish only if the sex drive was raised to a higher purpose. Lady Gregory disliked Maud, but feared for the effects of this sad and life-denying strategy. She urged him to propose to Maud — who had all but proposed to *him* — before she returned to Paris. He tried, on the eve of her going. When Maud turned him down, Lady Gregory told him, "Follow her to Paris. Court her, make love to her. Let yourself go. I'll pay for the trip." When he would not go, Lady Gregory offered to go to Maud herself to play *entremetteuse* and set up the wedding.

He told Lady Gregory, with that strangeness that was natural to him, "I am the fifty-ninth swan." He had counted them on the lake at Coole Park, her estate in Galway. There were always fifty-nine, not one more or less. Yet swans mate for life, so the count should have arrived at an even number. The poet saw his counterpart in the swan that was unmated, in a shared vocation for unhappiness.

He tells himself he is willing to accept his loneliness as the price that a terrible daimon has exacted for his creative power. But since he spurned Maud's juicy and magnificent dream, the poet in him, as well as the man, has been all but sterile.

So tonight, as the candles flicker in the great blue sconces, he reads to his guests from *The Wind in the Reeds*, the book of poetry that was printed a year before. In many of these verses, the mood is sad and slow. His voice, which can soar like a bird, or carry you far out to sea in wave upon wave of lovely sound, is tonight uncertain.

He embarks on a poem titled "Aedh Pleads with the Elemental Powers." He pronounces the Irish name *Ay*, to rhyme with *hay*. He is interrupted by a coughing fit that leaves him bent over.

"Who's Ay?" Van Meter demands, quite roughly, during the disruption.

Lady Gregory explains that in the stories of Ireland there are several gods and heroes with this name. "This Aedh is the Aedh of the Poets, called the comeliest of the gods. He is the brother of Aengus, the love god, and goes everywhere with a retinue of bards."

"Okay," says the American. "Then why not just call him the Poet? More people would get it and they wouldn't have to figure out how to pronounce funny-looking words."

"As our Irish goes," Lady Gregory contains the American, "Aedh is as easy a word as you may find."

"That's just my point!" Van Meter all but bellows. "Take a name like Cuchulain." He says something like "Ca-hooligan," and Lady Gregory briskly corrects him. "It's just too hard, unless you talk Gaelic, and how many people do that? Furthermore, it's out of date."

Yeats's other guests would not be surprised if he showed the American the door. But, still recovering from his spasms, he is mute as Lady Gregory speaks for both of them. "Cuchulain is a hero and a name of power. The Hound of Culain must have our respect, and that begins with giving him his rightful name, which is already a story. He is among those who sleep but may come again in our time of need. And it is only a poet who can raise him from his sleep, as the poets raised Fergus to recite the greatest of our Irish epics when the living had forgotten it."

Yeats clears his throat. He will try again to speak of the powers of wave and wind and windy fire, and the greater power that slumbers beyond all of these.

"The Polar Dragon slept," he reads.

His heavy rings uncoiled from glimmering deep to deep:
When will he wake from sleep?

His sickness betrays him. He can read no more. Lovely Florence offers her hand, and he gives her the open book, nodding acceptance. Her voice moves like moonlight on water as she completes the poem.

Encircle her I love and sing her into peace.

After Florence is done with the poem, silence hangs heavy in the room. Most of them know, or guess, for whom these lines were written.

Van Meter lights a cigar and breaks the silence. "Will we do some magic tonight, Mr. Yeats?"

It is Florence Farr's turn to be enraged. She and Willie have been engaged since the winter past in a magical battle. The Order of the Golden Dawn has broken into warring bands. From across the water in Paris, their former friend MacGregor Mathers is hurling poison words and magical darts. Closer and far more dangerous is the black sorcerer Crowley. Kilted like a Highlander with a black mask of an Egyptian god over his face, with a charter from Mathers in Paris and a posse of East End thugs, Crowley tried to bull his way into the Vault of the Order on Blythe Street and seize possession. Yeats himself stood at the head of the stairs, denying him entry until the police arrived.

In the war of magicians, Crowley's hired thugs and his license from Mathers are the least of his resources. He may be the most gifted magician in England. He casts a dark glamour that confuses and corrupts. He boasts of summoning things from swampy batrachian depths. Florence believes that Yeats may be ill because of the unremitting psychic attacks even more than because of his disappointments in love.

So this is hardly the night for magic, with the Order imperiled and outsiders in the room.

But once again the poet's response to Van Meter is mild. "What kind of magic do you have in mind?"

"Mimi and I saw some real bizarre magic in Paris. A Russian lady made flowers fall from the ceiling. They were swell, weren't they, Mimi?" His New Jersey countess smiles eagerly. "Roses, and orchids and dahlias, and all that good stuff. I paid extra to take them back to the hotel and everyone admired them. They gave me a vase for them. But in the morning, the flowers were gone. What do you think of that?"

"I say it was before the peacock screamed."

Van Meter rubs his chin. "Say again?"

"I believe Mr. Yeats is saying that we are quite familiar with this kind of magic in Ireland," Lady Gregory plays interpreter. "A man who walked in my own woods claims that he spent a night of feasting with the faeries. And in the morning he found that his mouth was full of grass and leaves."

"I really want to have an *experience* tonight," Van Meter persists. "Mr. Stead, don't you do manifestations in your séance shop?"

Stead's jaw is lengthened by a fierce growth of beard that is now aimed threateningly at the American. "If you are referring to our Bureau, I must tell you that its meetings are conducted according to the strictest rules of scientific evidence. We are neither Irish peasants — no disrespect, Lady Gregory — nor Cossack showmen. Our purpose is to open channels of communication to the Other Side, and to produce incontrovertible proofs that these contacts are genuine. We regard this as a vital public service."

"How so?"

"Because there are *many* people on the Other Side who urgently want to talk to the living."

"Then why don't they talk to us now?"

"I believe they would, if we only gave them room," Dorothea speaks up. "Is that not so, Mr. Stead?"

"It may very well be as Mrs. Hunter suggests. That is why it is necessary to arrange a controlled environment. If — ah — excarnates are all about us, then we don't want to invite just anyone in. It would be like Yeats leaning out the window at closing time and inviting all the drunks and floozies and cutpurses spilling out of the pubs to come and join the party. You would certainly get takers, but they would not likely be the guests you want, and it might not be so easy to persuade them to leave."

"I am a practical man," says Van Meter. "I trust what I can see and touch. Your séance room experiments *do* produce physical demonstrations, don't they?"

"The medium's voice and appearance may alter greatly, to be sure. She may speak in a language she does not know, as her vocal cords are manipulated by something outside herself."

"Apparitions, doubles, spirit resin? What do they call it — ectoplasm?"

"Sometimes. Such phenomena are aspects of what we call materialization."

"And how does that work, exactly?"

"A materialization is built up from the energy of the medium, or that of the whole circle."

"Can we do it now?" Van Meter looks hungrily from Stead to their host.

"I'm not at all sure we are prepared," Stead demurs.

"What more do you need, beyond a darkened room and a circle of people holding hands and bending their minds to the same purpose, if it is on the square?"

"Mr. Van Meter, the Bureau is accustomed to working through trained and dedicated mediums. Some of the best of our mediums are Americans, as you must surely be aware. Though most of us in this room may be counted as highly *sensitive*, we lack a medium in the professional sense."

"But didn't Mrs. Hunter suggest we can *all* be mediums? For sure, we all know *someone* on the Other Side. What do you say, Lady Gregory?"

"In Ireland, my servants and tenants see the dead as plainly as you can see me. We know very well in Ireland that there is no distance at all between this world and the Otherworld."

"So why don't we go for it?"

"We are guests of Mr. Yeats," Stead points out.

"I have no objection," says the poet, lighting another cigarette.

Thirty minutes' walk from Yeats's rooms in London, a rather different script is being enacted. In a cavernous room whose colors are all black and red. In the light of black and red candles, a hulking man wearing a black mask with Egyptian features stands with a curved blade at the apex of a triangle.

His acolyte approaches him, offering a trussed London pigeon in his cupped hands. The sorcerer cuts the pigeon's throat with the knife, then slashes at its breast, shaking blood over the point of the triangle. The Master Therion — as he wishes to be called — moves counterclockwise to the next apex and repeats the bloodletting. When he has killed the third pigeon, he considers his triangle *charged*. The blood will attract and help to provide an energy body for the powers of the Abyss he is calling in.

He has done this kind of thing, he believes, since very ancient times, in a succession of bodies that he has used and discarded like the robe he now wears. He knows there is nothing like blood (blood of sacrifice or blood of menses) to draw the forces he wishes to summon and direct, except for semen. The naked woman who hangs in a special harness on the wall, so devised that her head and limbs make the form of an inverted pentacle, will help him to provide both kinds of fluid.

Yeats and his guests are gathered around the table, holding hands.

"I feel a presence," says Dorothea, who has the sight by nature and has volunteered to act as medium. "It is like a druid king. His eyes are hard and cold. He will not speak to me. He is here for *you*, Frater." She calls Yeats Frater because he is her brother in the Order, as Florence is their sister.

Dorothea's eyes roll up, and her voice shifts to a deeper register.

"Go back and seal the doors. Do not come again until you come *armed*."

The rest is lost in a great cold river of wind that comes crashing and storming through the room. In Dorothea's sight, it rushes from a source in a frozen waste beyond the margins of the world she knows.

The unnatural wind grows denser and stronger, constantly shifting direction, twisting like a whirlwind. And it *howls*. The howl is not of a single voice, but of a legion of foul and violent things. "Have we called in the Wild Hunt?" Lady Gregory gasps. If there are human cries among the awful cacophony, they can only be the cries of the *sluagh*, the evil ghosts.

The evil wind carries all before it. The guests are spilled from their seats like dolls overthrown by a child in a tantrum. Books and glasses are hurled against the walls. The table is flung against the fireplace like a matchbook.

Yeats hangs on the wall above the divan, his legs shaking like willow branches.

He is looking into the face of the Abyss.

He is trying to say the *hekau*, the formal words of the Temple used to invoke the presence and the power of the gods. But his vocal cords will not work, and a terrible cold is moving into his bones and along the rivers of his blood. He feels that when he ceases to shake, he will no longer be able to move or speak at all.

He wills the Sword of Light into his hand, and tries to move his hand to make the banishing pentacle in the air. His arm is thrown back against the wall, and his hand flaps down, limp and useless, as if it has been nailed at the wrist.

When will he wake from sleep?

A woman's voice is calling and keening. Is it Florence who is singing? Or Dorothea? More than one woman, calling from more than one place. A warm shiver of hope and recognition streams through the poet's body, slowing the advance of the killing cold. His own words are sung, and other songs, of birds and rivers and trees. The words are flying like birds from tree to tree and peak to peak, through the Seven Woods and over the Golden Mountain, across the world and from world to world.

The women are calling a Power he has named.

It is coming not only for them, but for the world.

He is no longer hanging on a wall in a London apartment. He is hanging in a field of stars. From a distant star, a being that might be a female centaur, or a goddess, or both, raises a great bow of light and fits a shining arrow to the string.

The fiery arrow streaks across the sky, curving downward toward its mark in time.

You are the arrow I fired from my bow.

These are not the poet's words, and they are not for him, but may be for all. With her own sight, Dorothea sees *this*:

In a far past or a remote future, a circle is gathered, much greater than their own. Here beings who glow like candle flames are enthroned around a purple fire, the fire of a great jewel that burns with a purple flame. They are chanting. Their chant reaches down into the fiery heart of Earth, and rises to the stars.

Within the circle, raised on a bier, is a dead man, wrapped in bands of linen like a mummy.

The flamelike beings reach into the purple fire. With fanning motions, they transfer warmth and light into the dead man's heart, and his loins, and all the openings of his body.

As they continue to fan, a great winged shadow swoops down through the open roof of their castle or temple and vanishes under the mummy clothes.

The dead man begins to stir. As he strains for breath, the fabric of the shroud is sucked back into his moving jaws. His legs are kicking and thrashing. He rolls off the bier and turns over and over. The grave garments are peeling away.

The dead man is rising, fierce and magnificent, in the shape of a warrior king.

A woman's voice streams through the many voices:

"I will lead him out of death. I will send him into battle."

The heat is rising, rising. The frigid power that invaded the room in London hisses like ice turning to steam. The blood flows, hot and strong, in all of them. Now they can stand together again, joining hands and voices in a wordless chant that echoes the song of people of flame.

The howling returns and opposes them, but its terror is turning into a paroxysm of frustration and defeat. Dorothea sees the Adversary for a moment as a humanoid figure, naked and bald and bulging, with the eyes of a demented goat and a huge and hideous penis shaped like a club. It is flailing and thrashing in the immense talons of a power that none of them can see clearly, because this power is everywhere at once.

The howl recedes into the distance, and is joined by the raging scream of a man whose demons have been sent back.

They are all sweating; even Lady Gregory is glowing. Van Meter has thrown off his jacket. The poet is actually ruddy. He notices that the women are flushed and their lips are very red, but this seems right and good.

"Will someone tell me what the hell just happened?" says the American.

"Here we are, in the coils of the Dragon," Augusta Gregory all but croons.

"Is this normal in your séances, Mr. Stead?"

"At the Bureau? Hardly. You may wish to ask Yeats whether this is normal in his soirees."

Yeats has often wondered, in the séance room and in experiments in deep magic, whether the presences that appear to him, directly or through other vehicles, are other than projections of his own imagination. Of course, the imagination works real magic, and the stronger the imagination, the less imaginary its effects. He is certain that he did *not* imagine what came through tonight, not in the sense of making something up out of his own head. If what happened was imagined, it was the work of the mind of something other than a man living in London in the year 1900.

It occurs to him that what imagined the Dragon might be the entity with which he struggles incessantly, the power that constantly drives him to the hardest work among that which is not impossible. An entity that is and is not himself. He calls it his daimon.

His diaries are filled with his speculations about this daimon. It lives in the magical name he chose for himself within the Order. *Daemon est Deus inversus.* "The daimon is God inverted." He wonders now whether that is a correct statement. It is certain that, whatever it is, the daimon escapes all of his words.

He needs to know — one of many mysteries — how the daimon shapes or misshapes his relations with others, especially the women. Does the daimon also influence or facilitate a connection with people he does not know in his present time, people from the far past, or the remote future, like the warrior king that Dorothea saw raised from the dead? Through the daimon — or within an even greater entity of which the daimon is only a part — is it possible for selves separated by time or death to join each other in a common cause or a shared passion?

As his guests leave, Lady Gregory thanks him for a memorable evening and reminds him that he is welcome at Coole Park in any season. "It does you good, to walk in the Seven Woods and visit the wild swans and dream in the library, Willie. Come back to Coole whenever you please. It will always be your home."

2

She comes to him again, hovering over the bed. Clothes fall away. Without direction, without physical touch, his lower body undulating rhythmically, in a kind of horizontal snake dance, as she moves above him. As the serpent power rises, he rises with her, into midair and into a breezy space aflutter with gauzy fabrics and drapes, on a high hilltop.

Some days he feels her beside him, as he walks by a lake or reads aloud from his verse. She sends him letters, reporting her impressions of him from afar and suggesting astral assignations, most often at the holy places of Ireland but once at the casino in Aix-les-Bains. She does not speak of the winged, incandescent nights when the daimon is with him and in her, and they make love with a force that is surely more than human. She does not write of those mornings when he wakes to find her lying next to him as he stirs from sleep, and his heart leaps with joy until she fades like a wraith and he finds himself alone, aching to hold her and love her with all of his senses.

Now the poet is again among his guests, on another evening in his rooms off Tavistock Square. "There is no limit," he declares "to the power of *excited thinking*." He indicates a chessboard on the table. "Look at these chessmen. If we could but bring our thoughts to the necessary pitch of *trained* excitement, we could make them rise up and breathe and flourish their swords or scepters, and carry our news and our wills wherever we choose."

"You are talking of Egyptian magic, then," says one of his visitors.

"The secret is not peculiar to Egypt alone. It was done in Ireland, in the days of the high king Finn and the great king Cormac, with life-size chessmen on a green field large enough for hurling on the high holy hill of Tara."

"Now you are talking poetry. That is your privilege, of course. But my interest is in what works."

"Nothing works better than poetry." The new voice is a woman's. She stands tall and noble and shapely in the doorway, under a glory of burnished hair, her cape streaming from her shoulders. She is holding a lion on a leash. No, it is a huge lion-colored dog, a Great Dane, with the name of an Irish god. She looses Dagda, and the great dog leaps joyfully into Yeats's arms, licking his face until the drool runs down his chin and dampens his floppy silk tie. The poet extricates himself and mops his skin and clothes with a handkerchief, laughing. His pallor is gone. In the presence of this woman, shining like the sun, he is ruddy and full of juice. He cannot wait to get rid of his guests.

When they are alone, he explains the ritual he wishes them to perform together. It will be a holy thing, he tells her, and she consents without hesitation. While he waits for her to robe herself for their ceremony, taking her time as any woman might — let alone a queen among women — Yeats's eyes travel to an engraving he has hung above and a little to the right of the mantelpiece. It shows a swirl of naked figures, hurled along in a violent river of wind. They might be a flock of starlings wheeling in the sky, bound to a common purpose. They might be the train of the Wild Hunt. Some seem to be drowning, others dragged against their will, others simply whirling and turning, through loops of endless repetition. The whole pattern, viewed from across the room, resembles the coils of a monstrous serpent.

In a second slipstream, two figures whirl together, hands joined, eyes forever adoring each other. A heavenly light shines on them, but they are outside it. Beneath them, in a dead faint, lies Dante in a robe that is the red of desire. Standing over him, waiting for him to recover himself, is his guide, the poet Virgil, wearing the blue of memory and imagination.

Blake drew his inspiration for this disturbing picture from the Fifth Canto of Dante's *Inferno*, where the Italian poet described the fate of those who gave themselves to lust. The two lovers who stream forever together are Francesca and Paolo, who loved each other despite their marriage bonds, and were murdered by Francesca's jealous and misshapen husband. The story must be known in Italy, Yeats supposes, as that of Lancelot and Guinevere is known in these islands. It moved Dante to such pity that he fell on the ground like a dead man.

E caddi come corpo morto cade.

"I wonder that you keep that thing on your wall. You are hardly a product of the medieval church."

Yeats turns to look at her. She is magnificent in the green-gold silk that reveals more than conceals her shapes.

"Ah, but I fear I may be damned, not for the passion I have

lived but for that which is denied its consummation. I envy Paolo and Francesca, you see."

"Forever swirling, and churning."

"But they had each other. And still do. I would rather be in hell with you, than without you."

He is on his knees before her, and she is proud enough to enjoy the moment. Then she reminds him of her conditions. There will be no penetration, no emission, no release. These, she reminds him, are from the Order's rules of ceremonial magic. He accepts, yet is tormented by the idea that she is withholding herself because he disappointed her before.

He shares his vision of a new Celtic order, a knightly affair with its own castle on a lake. They perform the ritual, intended to charge the vision of power so it will take root in the world. The poet considers the magical operation a success, but as a man he is desperate, thwarted. He fears he will sicken again as he has done in the past when denied sexual release.

He cannot refrain from voicing his reproaches as they take tea together. "You told me once that you dreamed we were brought together by an Irish god. Yet you take up with rough brutes."

"I am of Ireland, Willie. And I am wedded to her cause."

"You are an English colonel's daughter."

"And my enemies make use of that, as you well know, hinting that because of my father I cannot be a Fenian and cannot be trusted. You know I am all the more Irish because I *choose* to be. As you have chosen, my dear man. Have you not dreamed me — do you not dream me — as the goddess of Erin herself?"

"I worship the goddess in you, my love."

"You are not Cuchulain, Willie. You are the Dragon even less. You are a beautiful man, and the greatest poet of our age, perhaps of any age, and your singing can help him to come again. But you are not the one."

"I trust you will not mistake some rough brute of a gunman for the Dragon."

"He must be a warrior. The world is at stake."

"The world is more than Ireland."

"Yes, but Ireland is its heart, and it is Ireland I must marry."

"Must you choose Ireland over *us*?"

"You are not the one, Willie."

He wants to fall to the ground at her feet, like Dante at the feet of Francesca, out of pity for himself but also for fear of what may become of her in a future he has seen. He has been shy and unconfident as a young man, but he has grown to know the pleasures of women's bodies, and to give pleasure — so they have intimated — in return. There will be many more women. He has seen them, face after face, in the Book of Life. One of them, as yet unknown to him, has shocked him in her photograph, sunbathing bare-breasted in a garden in France. Yet all his women, past, present, and future, will be only substitutes for *this* one, in *this* created world.

Coll was a poet, and the island folk said he was mad: but this was only because he loved beyond the reach of his fate.

The line, from a story by Fiona Macleod, runs through his mind. He sent her the book that contained that story. Had she read that line and thought of him?

3

Seven odors, seven murmurs, seven woods.

He is walking in the Seven Woods, at Coole Park. He comes to the lake and sees that the swans have left sky and water and settled in a green meadow. Across the distance, they look like tufts of sheep's wool. He can get near to them, perhaps, by crossing a field of cows. As he hoists himself over the stile, a red bull leaves the cows to challenge him, head down, steaming and potent, warning him away from his harem. Then the bull gets his scent and turns from him, shaking his rump, as if to say, *You are no competition.*

He knows already what the count will reveal. There are fifty-nine swans on the grass, as there were fifty-nine on the water last time he checked. Today he can identify the fifty-ninth swan, the lone one. He watches a mated couple drive the unpaired swan away with the noise of muffled bugles. He sees the solitary swan struggle through the wet grass. Clumsily, working pinions, he tries to lift off the ground. Perhaps his feathers are wet. It seems so hard for him to get airborne. Finally he wings his way above the lake toward the fairy hills, graceless and unloved.

The poet flies with him, sharing his pain. Swans are not meant to live alone. He knows the mate he would have if only she would have him. In the stories he has gathered from the peasantry, and from old books, gods and heroes alike may turn into swans, or be forced to take their shapes under a curse. The love god Aengus, no less, must shapeshift into a swan to find and win the lady he desires, when she flies at Samhain in the company of swans, in their form, to be recognized by the golden chain round her neck.

He wills himself, climbing higher, into the clouds, to find her spirit in a place of brightness. He couples with her in midair. He falls on her as Zeus comes to Leda. He will make this more than fantasy by carrying the lovely spirit he makes his above the clouds down to the body she has given to a red brute of a man, so that she may wake from his spell and leave his cattle field and come to the poet in the green meadow. What good is his magic without this?

Lady of Changes

Oracles have their own life, and can call you even when you are not calling on them. I took up the study of I Ching because Einstein met me at a Chinese gate and instructed me that the Chinese oracle is the best working model of the universe that is generally accessible. Months later, on a snowy night in a motel in western New York, the oracle came alive for me. Jung knew something of this. He wrote that "one could even define the I Ching oracle as an experiential dream, just as one can define a dream as an experiment of a four-dimensional nature."*

Her face glows in the dark of my bedroom like a golden moon. The lovely young Chinese woman is studying me intently. She is

---

*   Letter to the Rev. W. P. Witcutt, August 24, 1960, in C. G. Jung, *Letters, Vol. 2: 1951–1961*, trans. Jeffrey Hulen (Princeton: Princeton University Press, 1976), 584–5. The Mawangdui text quoted here follows the translation by Edward L. Shaughnessy, *I Ching, The Classic of Changes: The First English Translation of the Newly Discovered Second-Century BC Mawangdui Texts* (New York: Ballantine, 1997), 203.

as near as the foot of my bed. Her eyes are both very dark and very bright, her hair is lustrous black, cut neatly at shoulder length to produce a helmet effect. She is wearing a yellow tunic dress, and I remember that in China yellow is the color of Earth.

She communicates her intention: to teach me the real I Ching. As I look in her eyes, I see they are like eight balls in constant rhythmic motion, displaying the eight trigrams that compose the essence of the Book of Changes, marrying in pairs to make the sixty-four hexagrams.

If this is a Lady of Earth, of the receptive power of K'un, where is her consort? I see him now, wearing a robe of deep blue silk, embroidered with what may be bronze dragons. He is a Lord of Sky, and I know he personifies Ch'ien, the Heaven of the Changes. His lower body moves, indistinctly, like that of a great serpent-dragon, its coils turning like a Möbius strip. I sense that his lower body interweaves with that of the lady.

I recall that according to tradition, the trigrams were invented by the dragon emperor Fu Hsi, drawing knowledge from Heaven, and that in certain Taoist temples Fu Hsi and his consort Nuwa are depicted together. Their upper bodies are human; their lower bodies are those of serpent-dragons, intertwined. Awed by the energy presence of these ancient beings in my space, I am also embarrassed by my faulty memory of the Changes. I try to rehearse the names and forms of the eight trigrams in my mind. The primal pair: Heaven and Earth, Ch'ien and K'un. Fire and Water, Li and K'an. Lake and Mountain, Tui and Ken. Wind and Thunder, Sun and Chen. Do I have that right?

Not that way. The code of Thunder flares in the lady's changing eyes. Her fierce intent interrupts my effort to recite the list of the trigrams. *Like this.* Her eyes change again. I see a green mountain rising in a soft mist. There is a gentle lake at its summit, and around the peak a perfect cloud ring. Lake on the Mountain.

I struggle to remember the name and the attributions of the corresponding hexagram. Something to do with lovers, newlyweds, attraction.

Not like that. She is opening a different way of seeing and reading the code of the Changes. I relax into the embrace of Earth, and soon find myself in a different scene.

I am on top of a very tall and steep hill, with warriors dressed in skins and armed with bows and spears. There is an intense feeling of being alive up here. The wind is fresh and brisk, lifting my hair, fluttering a loose fringe. We may have a battle to fight, but our spirits are high, our defensive position is very strong, and we can see whatever is coming at us from far away. This hill fort has a commanding view. I can see across great vistas in all directions.

Access to our hill fort is via a wooden ladder that goes up the hillside for hundreds of feet. It can be pulled up to deny access to strangers. My traveling self is so agile that I doubt that he needs a ladder. Laughing, he sways his body over the edge of the drop until his back is almost horizontal. This defies human physiology. Maybe he has feet that can grip like fists. Respecting my human limitations, I take a step back from the brink, then smile at myself because the body I am using here can do things that the body I left in bed can't manage.

Remembering that my regular body is in a bed in a snowy town in western New York, I recollect my encounter with the lady who told me she would teach me the real I Ching. Am I inside one of the hexagrams? If so, which one? My guess would be the twentieth hexagram, which is called Kuan, or Watching. Wind over Earth.

The wind blows over the earth.
This is the image of Watching.
In this way ancient kings

looked across the four directions
observed the people
and gave them instruction.

I hang over the precipice, studying the ladder. Despite its great height, it has only six rungs. Now I recall that ascending the watchtower whose shape is concealed and revealed in the lines of the twentieth hexagram is a journey of six steps. Few can manage these six steps in the course of a lifetime. On the first step, we see as an unwise child; we notice only what relates to our cravings and fears. On the second step, we see like a nervous homebody peering out through a slit in a wall; protected by structure, we see little beyond it. On the third step, we look in a mirror and begin to observe ourselves, and what we have done and not done on our life journeys. On the fourth step, like lookouts, we can see across the land and provide news and warnings for our communities. On the fifth step, we return to self-observation, looking harder and deeper at our true selves. If we make it to the sixth and final step, we can see the whole. We can look at ourselves from a witness perspective. We no longer look from the ego, but from the greater Self.

Again, I see the changing eyes, with the turning codes, and sense the movement of the dragon coils in their Möbius dance. I have read thirty books on I Ching, and made my own guide to the hexagrams, giving personal names to each one and noting incidents that followed a particular reading on a certain date. I once taught a course titled "I Ching for Dreamers" in which we *drummed* the patterns of broken and unbroken lines, inspired by the most ancient, fragmentary text of the Book of Changes, found in a lacquer hamper in the tomb of a lord at Mawangdui as recently as 1973, where it is written that "the sages drummed the movements of all under Heaven" into the oracle.

However, I consider myself a rank amateur in this area, and would not trust my ability to read the Changes until I have internalized the sixty-four hexagrams and the changing lines without the need to look anything up. In Chinese tradition such mastery requires either a lifetime of training, memorizing, and practice or the direct inspiration of past masters, or both.

The shining eyes give me Heaven under Earth, the desirable placement since this means the primal pair are coming together. Maybe I can aspire to know a little more of the Changes in the years that remain to me. Maybe, with the Yellow Lady and the Blue Lord as gatekeepers, I will lead others on a journey through the cycles, to climb the ladder of six steps to the watchtower.

Ghost Platoon

Native Americans call it *ghost sickness*. It gets very bad when you are afflicted by ghosts of war who blame you for their deaths. In Vietnam, they speak of the angry ghost (*con ma*) who causes sickness. I've been required to help veterans who have come home from war carrying angry ghosts, even a whole platoon of them. They can not only make you sick in this world; they can show up in very unpleasant ways on the road to the next.

"Nice talking to you." Ian got up from the bar.

"What's your hurry?" asked the man on the next stool, over his martini. "They haven't called your flight yet."

"I'm going to the men's room."

"Are you sure about that?" The bartender, listening in, gave Ian a strange look as he shook a cocktail shaker.

"If it's okay with you."

Martini man laughed so hard he spilled some of his drink. The bartender refilled his glass from the shaker at once, as if he

knew the spill was going to happen. They were very strange people, in the Parting Glass. Maybe it was the effect of rolling delays,
and the transience of the locale, with the sense of being not off the
ground and yet no longer quite on it.

Ian is walking through the food court. He hears the bad talk of a
couple who are having a full-blown fight. The woman has discovered something on a cell phone. She screams, then breaks down
and sobs. The man crumples and mutters an apology. Then it
starts again. The woman looks at the cell phone and screams, as if
a replay button has been pushed.

The pattern is repeated in the gift shop. A little boy plucks a
stuffed penguin from a rack. His mother tells him she's not going
to buy it, and he throws it on the floor. His mother puts it back.
He pulls it from the rack and throws it on the floor again.

The men's room is tucked away in a narrow hall, behind a
janitor's closet.

Ian has the place to himself until he starts washing his hands.
He jumps when a burly man in military uniform looms up behind him in the mirror.

"Second Lieutenant Ian D. Forrester."

"Nobody's called me that for a long time."

"They're waiting for you."

"Who?"

"Charlie Company Two."

Ian wheels around. The soldier is not in the restroom. Behind
where he stood, there is no wall. The space opens into a fetid jungle. The smell of rot and burning blows into the space on a foul
wind. It seizes Ian like a giant fist and pulls him into the last place
he wants to be in any world.

The tops of the trees are burning. Hundreds of feet below, Ian
is pushed and pummeled over slippery ground in a suffocating,
acrid fog.

Forms rise from the fog and slide between the trees. They squeak and twitter like bats.

Who's in charge?

He is not sure whether this voice is inside his own mind or coming from the fog.

A thing like a broken umbrella, man-sized, raises up from a muddy hole. It shambles toward Ian and hisses graveyard breath into his face. The eye sockets are dark and vacant.

Other things are coming out of the ground. They are rising out of the foxholes that failed to give any real protection — Ian remembers now — against the cannons and mortars of the North Vietnamese army. One of the walking dead is hoisting himself out of his bunker with the stubs of the fingers he lost to shrapnel.

Who's in charge?

There is a terrible repetitive sound from deep in the earth. It is something like a creaking door, and something like an old tin roof banging in the wind. Ian does not care to know what is coming with it. He remembers how the enemy exploded out of tunnels he had been assured could not be there — an enemy in the uniforms of the Northern army as well as in the black pajamas and rubber-soled sandals of the Cong.

The energy of his fear gives him strength to break free from his captors. He runs, forgetting his age and his bum knees, toward the hillside he ordered his platoon to clear for the choppers.

He listens for the whirring blades of a Huey, willing his rescuers to come. He hears something above the terrible thumping and creaking from inside the earth. At first, it sounds like a bee trapped inside a window. As it grows louder, Ian dares to hope.

He remembers how he stood at this exact spot, crouched over the wounded boy he had dragged here, firing the last clip of his M-16.

A quaking aspen looms out of the fog. No, it's a young soldier, nearly seven feet tall.

"Tiny?"

It's the boy Ian dragged to the helicopter pad. He was a sweet-faced kid from the Midwest, not too bright but a great hoop player, who never held a grudge. He gave Ian a letter to send to his sweetheart, while trying to hold his intestines inside the hole a Northern shell had punched in his gut.

Tiny is smiling now.

No, that isn't a smile, just the rictus of death where flesh has rotted from the bone.

Ian backs away from the grinning skull. The whirring is louder, but it is not the sound of a helicopter. More like a swarm of huge flying bugs.

Who's in charge?

"Shut up!" Ian yells at the mad voice.

Twenty-two dead men. Count them.

They are forming a circle around him, moving in toward him.

Who's responsible?

Ian calls out, "I'm sorry! I did everything I could!"

What kind of officer gets all his men killed and goes home without a scratch?

"It's not my fault I didn't die!"

The response is demented laughter.

"Tiny? You know I tried to get you out. And I delivered your letter. I took it to Indiana myself."

Did you try to fuck his girl?

"Shut up!"

"Sarge?" He appeals to what might be the refrigerator bulk of his platoon sergeant, a career soldier from Baltimore who never ducked a fight or an obligation.

The walking refrigerator emits a sighing, sawing sound that makes Ian queasy.

Dead eyes. They all have dead eyes, whether or not the eyeballs are missing. There is no mind here, no consciousness, nothing of soul. Just a terrible appetency, and a reaching for revenge.

Ian sees now that each of them has a weapon.

Wallensky — if that is truly the radio man — is crackling with electricity, darting miniature lightning bolts from his fingers.

Halston, who could never be kept away from a bottle, is spitting blue fire, like a sputtering human flamethrower.

Sarge's weapon is more conventional — a bayonet held by an arm as rigid as a rifle. This fills Ian with particular horror, because it reminds him that before he died screaming, Sarge was clutching a gushing red hole in his groin. Whatever is driving Sarge's hand, Ian has no doubt where the bayonet is being aimed.

The whirring and rustling of the still-unseen swarm is beating up a terrible wind.

Ian abandons hope of reasoning or pleading with the mind-gone men of his ghost platoon, the twenty-two men he lost in a battle for a nameless hill the day before his twenty-second birthday. How long ago was that? Why, after all the years, are these men not at rest?

He now remembers a scared chopper pilot who would not go down for the bodies. They called in another napalm strike instead, heedless of the fact that the chemical fire rarely made it all the way down to the ground. They flew back with black rubber body bags in the back of the Huey, unused. At the base, they tried to calm him with whiskey and tokes and force-fed him a T-bone steak until he puked his guts out. Then they drove him to the airport, through a city that smelled of rotting fish, and put him on a plane to Bangkok for some R&R before flying him back to Washington to receive a medal he knew he did not deserve.

He feels a huge weight over his heart, and realizes he is wearing that medal, on the ribbon that was slung around his neck in front of the honor guard.

That can't be right.

How's it feel to be a hero? The mad voice mocks him.

The dead men grab and clutch as he barrels through their line, stumbling and falling down the hillside toward the village.

Above him, the tops of the trees are burning. Below, through the clearing fog, he sees a waterlogged landscape. The village is closer than he remembers. Soon he is sloshing through rice paddies toward a ramshackle collection of stilt houses on the banks of a sluggish, swampy river.

Children gather to watch him. Their faces are hollow, their bellies distended with hunger.

Ian struggles to remember why he came to this village.

The Rice Denial Program, they called it. In the name of something called "pacification," his unit was ordered to come to this village and confiscate its reserves of rice, to prevent them from falling into enemy hands. The rice was to be delivered to the forces of the pro-American government, which might or might not return it to the villagers. Looking at the starving children, Ian sees what the policy became in practice.

The children's mothers and sisters are flirting with him from doorways. Some of them pull down their tops or their pajama bottoms to show him what they are offering. One bolder than the rest rubs against him, pressing her hand between his legs, darting her tongue between her lips.

Before he knows how, he is in a room with her, and his pants are down. She is milking him with her mouth, except her head is no longer where it was. Her body parts have switched, so her face is where her bottom was.

He stumbles screaming from the stilt house, trying to pull up his pants. He trips and falls down the ladderlike steps, landing facedown in the stinking mud. When he rolls on his back, girls and women are all around him. They are naked, their limbs like sticks. Their eyes are not dead in the same way as those of his ghost soldiers. There are razor blades in the pupils.

Kill the pig! Kill the pig! The chorus is coming from everywhere.

It squalls above a buzzing that is closer than the sound of what he had hoped was a rescue helicopter. This time the buzzing is coming from little bamboo boxes and cages all the women are holding. He cannot see what is inside, and does not want to see.

Kill the pig! Kill the pig!

He staggers toward the swollen river. Its waters are poison green and rust brown, alive with nasty black things that may be leeches. Some of the women run in front of him, but they do not try to head him off. Rather, they form lines on either side, so he is moving through a tunnel of distorted flesh. He has the impression that the soldiers of the ghost platoon are gathering behind the women. The buzzing grows unbearably loud. He presses his hands to his ears, trying to shut it out, but it is coming from inside as well as outside his head.

A tremendous bellowing, bugling sound cuts through the buzz. All other noises are stilled, except for a grunting and stamping that sends a mess of mud and shit spattering Ian's face and chest, followed by the repetition of that bellowing roar.

Kill the pig, kill the pig! The chant resumes.

Ian sees the swollen shape ahead of him, huge and ungainly as a hippopotamus. The little piggy eyes blazed with a killing fury. The stamping hooves and the great heaving belly churn the sodden earth, driving the mud into ridges and valleys in which Ian flounders to keep his balance.

Who's in charge? The mad voice mocks him again.

Only now does he understand who is speaking, and what confronts him.

Who's in charge?

It is his own desperate voice, but it carries from a different time. It is the shout of a subaltern who is not quite twenty-two and has lost control of his men, who are losing their minds before they lose their lives.

The muddy, fevered scene around him shudders and changes. The people around him no longer have the eyes of the dead. The boar is no longer at the riverbank.

Ian Forrester is in the body of a young man whose lieutenant's tabs do not buy him much respect from his men. They are hungry and scared and sex-starved. Some are doped to the eyeballs. Only Sarge is a pro, a regular Army man. The rest are conscripts, pushed into this green hell at a time when nobody believes in this war.

They roll into the village in their jeeps whooping and singing. Some of the men are bawling "Puff the Magic Dragon" like the hotshot chopper jockeys. They may be hoping that if they make enough noise, the Cong will vanish until after the raid.

This is a rice-denial mission, but the villagers don't have much surplus rice, at least not for Americans to find. The bags have probably gone down into the tunnels along with the Cong — the tunnels that are too narrow for a stateside soldier's shoulders, on the rare occasions when one is detected.

The men make a house-to-house search. Only women and children and ancient men with a few wispy hairs on their chins seem to be left in the village.

Screams erupt from one of the houses. Moran is so wired he squeezes off a round involuntarily, shooting himself in the foot.

Ian unholsters his .45 and runs toward the place of the screaming. There is a burst of gunfire from inside. The screams continue. Ian pushes through the bead curtain. A young woman lies in a darkening pool on the floor, with a zigzag pattern of bullet holes across her chest. The screams are coming from Kravchuk, who is clutching himself, trying to stop the fountain of blood that is gushing through his hands.

"Fucking razor girl," spits Marconi, the soldier who shot the girl. "She gave us the come-on, I swear."

"Corpsman!" Ian instructs the medical orderly to stitch up Kravchuk as best he could.

Word gets around fast that there are assassins among the villagers, that you can't distinguish them by age or sex.

Now all the men are scared, and many of them want something to kill.

That's when they find the food supply: a giant belly-dragging boar, in a special enclosure.

"That's enough hog for a month of barbecue," says Sarge admiringly.

The giant is a sow, and its swollen teats suggest that it's carrying piglets. One of the wispy-bearded ancients kowtows, and explains through a kid with broken English that the boar is a sacred pig, that it contains all the good fortune of the village.

"Hey," says Marconi, "it's picnic time." He raises his M-16.

"Put your weapon down, soldier."

"Aw, come on, lieutenant. We're supposed to deny food to these commie gooks."

"Who's in charge here?" Ian demands. "There's no need to kill their pig."

Kill the pig, kill the pig! Ian can't tell where the chanting starts. Soon most of the men have joined in.

"Who's in charge?" he yells above the racket.

He is fatigued, and dizzy with heat and fever. Marconi shoots the boar. It squeals and comes down on the wall of the enclosure, splintering and scattering beams and slats. It writhes on its back, merely wounded.

There is only one thing for Lieutenant Forrester to do. He kills the pig. He empties his clip to be certain the great beast is dead.

The boy translator stands in front of Ian, speaking for the old man.

"You have a curse on you now. It will never go away."

The earth shudders again, all the shapes blur into a muddy, greenish haze, and now Ian is again within the gauntlet of the dead, before the beast, with the men of the ghost platoon shuffling toward him from behind.

He looks across the river. There is a boat on the water, near the farther shore. In the boat is a beautiful woman in blue, with a large black dog.

The dog reminds Ian of many dogs he has loved, especially of one he buried on a rainy night when he felt his heart was breaking. There is something familiar about the woman in blue. Is that a flight attendant's uniform she is wearing?

The dog splashes into the water and starts swimming toward him.

And there is a change in Ian.

"I'm in charge," he says softly, speaking to the dead. Then louder, "I am responsible!"

He turns in a slow circle, surveying the walking dead.

"But I do not have to answer to *you*," he says with absolute conviction. "You are not my judges. You are not *real*. You are just — leftovers."

He walks deliberately forward, toward the open jaws of the great slavering beast.

Courage is not the absence of fear, he recalls. It is the willingness to step through the fear.

The jaws of the giant boar open wide as a castle gate. Ian

steps into it. The jaws close behind him, and he is in a pulsing darkness, blacker than black. The passage dips and narrows. He is sucked down into a maelstrom of churning acids. His flesh is being stripped from his bones. Good. He is happy to part with his old man's body, with its cargo of pain and guilt.

He is scraped and purged and polished.

He is hurled toward something like a trapdoor that opens and shoots him out across the river.

The current is strong, but the black dog meets him.

Ian clings to his collar and kicks as hard as he can. They are skimming the water, swimming easily to the boat, where the woman in blue smiles as Ian climbs on board.

As she holds out a soft blue blanket, he is embarrassed to find he is naked. And also astonished that his body is no longer that of an old man with arthritis and liver spots. His body is strong and supple and lightly tanned, the body of a young man who is no stranger to sun and sea.

"You did the right thing," the woman in blue brushes away the questions he is trying to formulate. "You were misled, but it came out for the best, because you realized you do not belong with the dead."

"But aren't I — I mean — "

"Certainly not. Your body is dead, but that is only meat. Now you have left your body bag behind too, in the belly of the beast."

"Body bag?"

"Oh yes, there is a body that survives the ordinary body. But you can't take it with you anywhere you would want to go. If you get stuck in it, you are condemned to the realm of the hungry ghosts."

Ian looks toward the village and sees the ghosts sniffing after him, squeaking and twittering on the shore. They seem afraid and perhaps unable to enter the water.

Ian notices the silver wings on her lapel. "You're from the airline. You're — "

"Come this way, please. We'll be boarding soon."

The airport is different now. There is a silver glow to everything. Movement around him has stopped. He follows the woman in blue along an air bridge. The cabin door is open. Inside everything is suffused with a lovely blue light.

Mircea on the Isthmus

I grew up reading Mircea Eliade, the great Romanian scholar of religions who gave us the first major book on shamanism and wrote tirelessly in many genres, including fantasy. He regarded the journal as his ideal medium, as I do. I did not expect to have a personal interview with Mircea after his death, but it unfolded very much as described in this story when I was leading a retreat at a villa in Transylvania, where strange things happen all the time.

I was going to call this story "Eliade in the Bardo." Then George Saunders published his extraordinary novel, *Lincoln in the Bardo*, and I decided I must think again. I plucked the word *isthmus* from the writings of the great medieval philosophers of mystical Islam, notably Ibn 'Arabi, for whom the *barzakh*, or isthmus, is an intermediate realm, between body and spirit, between the visible and the invisible, between the human and the divine.

Spirits of the dead and the living meet and mingle on the *barzakh*, especially in dreaming. According to his student Sadruddin Qunawi, Ibn 'Arabi, as a master of the imaginal realm, "had the power to meet the spirit of any prophet or saint departed from this world, either by making him descend to this world and contemplating him in an apparitional body similar to the sensible form of his person, or by making him appear in dreams, or by unbinding himself from his material body to rise to meet the spirit."[*]

"Take your pick," the owner of the villa greeted me. "Any room you like. On this side" — he gestured toward the right side of the corridor — "you will hear the dogs at night, barking at the bears."

"And on the other side?"

"Only bears."

I had seen the dogs, as big as bears. I opted for a room on the side away from their kennels, where there was nothing between me and the bears.

Our group dined on *sarmale*, cabbage-wrapped ground meat and vegetables, and drank the black wine of the country. I sat outside after dinner under a nut tree and smoked a cigar, looking at Dracula's castle at Bran, in clear line of sight, with the snow-capped peaks of the mountains behind. Lucian, a storyteller of the kind Mark Twain would have appreciated, told me, "I know the people of this area very well. At weekends they go to the cemetery and open coffins. If a body has moved, they drive a stake through the heart."

"I take it television reception isn't good around here."

We all laughed. Jokes and tall tales about vampires are inescapable in Transylvania. They are essential to the tourist industry. However, as my Romanian friends readily agreed, it is not

---

[*]   Quoted in Henry Corbin, *Creative Imagination in the Sufism of Ibn 'Arabi*, trans. Ralph Mannheim (Princeton: Bollingen, 1981), 224.

the vampire that is quintessentially Romanian, but the werewolf and perhaps the werebear. Ancient Dacian warriors whipped themselves into battle frenzy under the banner of a wolf-headed dragon. I read in one of Eliade's early essays on Romanian folklore that Zalmoxis, a shaman-god of healing, was born in a cave and appeared as a bear before he transformed into a human.

I went up to my room early. I read some pages of Eliade's journals. I felt the grief of the exile who was never be able to return to his native country after the Second World War, when the Communists took power.

The silence of the mountains was broken only by the sound of dogs barking on the far side of the villa, too far away to bother me. I may have drifted off, because I sat up with a start when I heard an owl calling. Its screech was repeated, insistent, seemingly personal. I went out on the balcony and looked down on the steep slope of the hill, rising into the forest. Moonlight cast a moving circle on the damp grass, like a searchlight. A shadow moved with it. Mine? I waved my arm, and the shadow seemed to wave back. But wait: the shadow was moving the other arm. I was intrigued. I pulled on my shoes and padded down the stairs and through the dining room to a side door of the villa.

The shadow was waiting. It came to meet me as I walked across the grass. It seemed to be deep blue rather than black. It spread its arms, as I did, with recognition, not fear. I felt it fold itself around me like an indigo robe.

Now I was traveling, rising up into the air. The villa and the houses and fields around were laid out below, a living diorama. Soon they were smaller, in my vision, than the model-train sets I laid out on the floor of my bedroom as a boy. Soon Bran Castle was just a pinhead in the folds of the mountains.

I continued to rise, neither willing nor resisting. My strongest feeling was curiosity. I felt my ascent being aided by an intention beyond my own, as if I was being drawn by a gentle tractor beam — not required to stay within it, but invited. I turned, looked up, and saw a subtle architecture rising high above. Level upon level, separated by what might have been filmy cloud banks or translucent glass.

Squatting high above me, legs folded, his body hieratically arranged in what I took to be a yoga asana, was a man I thought I knew. I had admired his work as a scholar of shamanism and religion since I was an undergraduate. He had captured my imagination with his strange tales in which real people — under their real names — switch worlds. In Bucharest, I had visited places from his youth. On Mantuleasa Street, I stood under his statue, with its strangely blurred face, suggesting that he could not be contained in its form. I was leafing through one of his journals in bed before the owl called me out to meet the shadow.

It was hard to gauge perspective up there on the astral. I could not see the moon. It struck me that the figure high above me must be enormous to be visible to me, far below.

I was certain now that the giant floater was Mircea Eliade.

I called up to him. "Professor?"

A great eye opened, above and between his closed eyes, and the pupil swiveled to look down on me. This was horrible but fascinating. I cleared my throat.

"May I ask what you are doing up there?"

"You don't know much about yoga, do you?"

"Not really my thing. But I read your books."

"I am become Avalokiteshvara."

I thought this a little grandiose, but scaled to the form he had assumed. I knew the name. I recalled that Eliade in his prime had devoted years to the study and practice of yoga and Eastern traditions. *Avalokiteshvara* means "the lord who looks down upon the world." It is the name of a bodhisattva, an enlightened master who can create higher worlds, or dispense with them.

"I would like to talk to you," I called up to the floating professor. I resisted the urge to laugh; it occurred to me that he looked like a giant helium balloon. "Would you consider coming down so we can have a conversation?"

"You don't get to be where I am without paying a greater price than you can understand. Why would I want to descend to your level?"

"You look lonely up there." I knew I risked ending the encounter, but this statement seemed to me to be true, and I did not intend to crouch beneath his feet like the most abject of *chelas*. "Furthermore, you called me up here for a reason."

The terrible third eye gave me a withering glare. "What makes you think I called you?"

"If you had not called me, how could I have found you?"

The great body shook, in what might have been, in a mere human, a shrug of dismissal. This brought him out of the pose of cosmic detachment, so I knew he was coming down. He seemed to glide, pausing from time to time as if sledding down the ridges of one of the snow-capped mountains below us. As he fell, his third eye closed, his ordinary eyes opened, and he diminished to human scale. He showed himself now like the man recorded in photographs from midlife.

I expected him to make a statement about the meaning of everything, now that he had succeeded in fulfilling the greatest ambition of his former life: stepping out of the nightmare of history. Instead he said, "Do you have some tobacco?"

"I have cigars in my room."

He showed his disappointment. He used to smoke like a snake, as Romanians say — cigarettes in early life, pipes later on.

"Do you really miss tobacco?" I looked up to where he had been floating in his cosmic yoga position.

"Not up there," he said with some irritation. "I miss it down here, where you made me come to talk to you. Let's make an agreement. We'll go to your place, and you will smoke a cigar while we talk. It's only the smoke that I need. It's all in the smoke."

"Very well." I was nervous that we were going to lose contact as I dropped back into my body — in the bed, not on the grass — with a thump. I got my body up, gargled with mouthwash, and dressed in the warmest clothes I had brought, because the night had turned very cold. I walked down the corridor to the heavy glass door of the communal terrace, which had easy chairs and ashtrays and exercise machines. It was deserted at this hour. I threw myself back in a well-padded armchair, clipped and lit a cigar, and took a few long drags. I don't inhale. I'm not sure how Mircea, as a vapor eater, processed what I was puffing out.

He asked, "Where shall we begin?"

"I want to know all of your journey. You taught us how shamans and arhats travel the roads of the afterlife like theme parks."

"I never used those words."

"Well, the point is, you have taken those roads, and I would like to know what you have learned. And how you now see the life you lived before, which has inspired many but also left puzzles within mysteries."

"Blow more smoke this way."

For a moment, his face vanished in the blue-gray cloud. Then I was drawn into the cloud and through it. He had drawn me into his memories, of what happened when he left his body behind for the last time on this earth.

He has memorized the instructions for his ascent. He is armed with mantras he has recited a thousand times. He has the addresses of a dozen desirable destinations in the worlds of form, and a plan for ascending beyond worlds of form to a level where karma is canceled and time is abolished.

But he is challenged by menacing figures. Some of them seem

to be rising from open graves. He recognizes old enemies still full of hate. More terrifying are old comrades, some in the green uniforms of a lost cause, who batten onto him, flapping like moths. They are distracting him, dragging him down and back. If he goes with them, he knows they will carry him to a Land of the Dead, where he will lose his mind.

He wills himself to rise above them. His life has prepared him for this. He uses words of power. He calls on the celestial bird that has come to him in dreams and meditation. But he is still among the hungry ghosts.

He thinks of the color green, not the green of the Legionaries but of a green sanctuary full of light and sweetness. His thought is so strong it puts him back in the place of safety he found on a drowsy summer afternoon in a garrison town before he could walk. As an infant, he crawled into the drawing room of the family house and found it bathed in extraordinary light, filtered by the drawn heavy, green velvet curtains. Now, as then, he feels he is inside a huge green grape, a sweet and protected space. He rests inside, motionless with wonder. He looks for the beautiful face he saw all those years ago in the deep Venetian mirrors in the room, the face of a guide ennobled by the light of another world. But the skin bursts. He can't stay inside the green grape.

Now he is riding a streetcar in his old neighborhood in Bucharest. The grander houses have fan-shaped sun ports of frosted glass, high wrought-iron fences, curving drives, and manicured hedges. As the tram slows for the next stop, he sees *that* house, half-hidden by overgrown gardens, shaded by walnut trees. He gets off the streetcar, wiping his face with a handkerchief, because it is intolerably hot. The iron gate opens at his touch, and he stumbles along the garden path into dappled shade. The old woman is there, with a jug of something cool. She does not offer him a drink. She extends her palm. He remembers the price. Has it changed? Are the bills in his wallet still acceptable currency? There is a different face on the banknotes now, surely. The old woman takes the three bills from his hand and spirits them out of sight. Three bills for three girls.

"You go to the cottage," she instructs him. "You know what is required. You must pick the Gypsy girl."

He is trying to keep his head. He knows he is being tested, though surely he must win this game, since he invented it. The fate of the wretched piano teacher in his story is not for him. He does not have to guess at the identities of the three women who are waiting for him, displaying themselves like odalisques. He might be in the harem at the Topkapi palace in Istanbul, city of magic columns, in the age of sultans and pashas.

"You don't fool me," he tells them. "I created you. I created this cottage, this garden. I can make it vanish, and you with it, with a snap of my fingers."

They smile and weave a dance around him. The dark-haired one, bold and voluptuous, is naked except for her jewels. The blonde, lazy and rounded, is naked except for her veil. The red-head, slender as a gazelle, is naked under her diaphanous wrap. They all excite him. The threefold magic is working. The serpent is rising. He has always been proud of his potency. But this is fantastic. He is Priapus. From the threshold, he can reach them and tease them with the snake that is no longer in his trousers. He can flirt with their secret places, lick at the small of the back, at the crook of the elbows, at any pleasure point.

He feels like a tantric god. He is under them, over them, riding them, being ridden at a fast clip and then held almost immobile, standing like a magic column, like a fountain. They worship him with their moans and cries.

Then the fountain stops running. It stands tall, but the flow is cut off. His organ might have been turned to stone. At the same time, he is in acute pain. A great force is pressing for release, but cruelly blocked.

He swears at the girls. He threatens to vaporize them, reminding them that they are his creatures, born at his writing desk in the middle of the night.

"You have to guess," they taunt him. He must remember the game that the wretched piano teacher agreed to play in his story. He has to guess which of the three girls is the Gypsy. In the story, one of them is German — or Jewish — while the third is Greek — or is it Turkish? How could he have forgotten?

"You're all fucking Gypsies," he swears at them. "You're all thieves and deceivers!"

Their laughter hurts the ears, like a storytelling of crows, swooping and batting and pecking at him. He needs to get out of this astral trap he has made for himself out of lust and disordered imagination. He pulls up his pants and starts to retrace his steps. But when he moves to the door, he finds his nose up against a mirror. He changes direction and sees more mirrors with heavy drapes, like theater curtains, between them. He claws back the drapes and finds himself in a tunnel lined by hanging cloths that give no exit but confuse him as he is obliged to keep changing direction. He comes out at last in front of the mirror that had first rebuffed him. He sees an old man with a stubble beard, slump-shouldered, his flaccid organ hanging useless out of his fly.

He yells at this false universe, "I have mastered the *siddhis*! I know the *dharmata*! I have sat with Shivananda and made and unmade worlds! I have studied every path to the clear light, to the happy abodes of buddhas and the heavens of the gods and the island paradises of savages! You can't keep me in this prison of low illusions!"

In front of the mirror, he cannot escape the fact that he is shouting at himself. He steps through the mirror.

The scene outside has not changed. He walks the path through the overgrown garden, back to the street. A tram is right there, approaching the stop. He does not know what to do, because he recalls, with horror, that in his story the piano teacher became lost in time when he tried to take a streetcar home.

The conductor is calling to him, "Get on! We've come for you."

Not finding another way to escape this reality, he boards the streetcar. He can't fathom where it is going. The only address that comes to him is that of the squat corner building where he wrote through stifling summer nights as an adolescent — wonder tales and meticulous articles on the sex lives of insects for a science magazine. The memory comes of candles burning in front of the icons inside the church of St. Michael and St. Gabriel on Mantuleasa Street. How long has it been since he prayed in an Orthodox church? Can he now dare to ask for help from that quarter?

He starts to explain to the conductor where he now wants to go. The conductor, who has not asked for a ticket, tells him, "We know where you are going."

The streetcar stops in front of a cinema. It is almost the double of the cinema in Paris where he watched the new Disney film *Bambi* toward the end of the war, when it was clear that his country was lost. The atmosphere in that theater was thicker than the smoke from the cigarettes that everyone who could manage to buy them was smoking in 1944. The lovely landscapes and cute animations of the Disney studios were a welcome distraction from the war, from Nina's illness, from his neurasthenia and private agonies, which he tried to quell with drug after drug. On the screen, a talking doe warned Bambi to watch out because "man" was nearby. The whole audience held its breath, petrified — he felt — with shame and fellow feeling for the hunted animals. Everyone looked straight ahead. Nobody wanted to look at the person next to him, to see or be seen. The manager decided not to screen the newsreels after that.

The counterpart cinema where he now takes a seat has an unusual name: the Biograph. The theater seems to be deserted, but he soon has the impression that someone is sitting to his left. He does not turn. He looks straight ahead, as he did in Paris when the deer warned against man, and when he knew in his gut that the guilty would judge the guilty in a land to which he would never return, and that his wife was going to die.

When he got to Paris, he had lost his black notebook, with his most intimate confessions, on a train, and this had terrified him. He had torn certain other pages from other journals.

Now, in the Biograph, as the curtains are cranked back, and images begin to appear on the screen, he sees that he has not succeeded in expunging anything from a larger memory. They are playing newsreels of his life, days of joy and terror, moments of beauty and despair. He knows what game they are playing. They want him to make his own accounting, to weigh his own heart against the feather of truth. He does not want to play this game, but cannot turn his eyes from the screen. The technology here is brutal. To look at a scene is to be pulled inside it, without being able to submerge his critical awareness in the passions of his earlier self.

"That's what they do," Mircea said, as his face reemerged from the smoke on the terrace. A rooster crowed. "They make us sit in judgment on ourselves. I was made to live my whole past, dark and light, and be present to all of it. I was overwhelmed by guilt and disgust, then allowed a moment of joy and elation, then plunged into the most profound sadness. You must know what this is about."

"We must find a way to move beyond our regrets."

"We must find a way to forgive ourselves. There is no *they* in the end. We judge ourselves."

"Are there still things you regret?"

"When I look over my former life, my biggest regret was that I failed to become a bestselling novelist."

"Really? That still matters to you?"

"It was my great ambition, you know. I hoped I would fulfill it with the publication of the novel you know as *Bengal Nights*. But I failed. So I went on writing *Shamanism* in a garret in Paris, holding a bottle of hot water in my lap to thaw my hands in winter. And I suppose it has been of interest to some specialists."

"More than to specialists." I explained to him that his book, more than any other, had influenced a shamanic revival all over the world and provided essential models of understanding and vocabulary, starting with the word *shamanism* itself. "Your writings on religion and mythology have shaped so many minds, including mine. You gave so much to the world."

"But that path was my second choice. My first choice was to devote myself to literature. Who knows me in your time as anything other than a professor, a memoirist, perhaps the author of a few fantastic stories? Don't miss your own opportunity."

"In life, one of my greatest regrets was being separated from my books. After the war, I could not recover the personal library I assembled in Bucharest, using most of the money I managed to earn from small-circulation magazines or borrowed from friends. I lost more books in traveling from London to Lisbon to Paris to Chicago, and each time it felt as if friends had died.

"I see you share this attachment to books, the bibliophile's fever for possession, to be able to caress and stroke and penetrate with a pencil at any hour. I can give you a little comfort by telling you that on the Other Side you will find that this attachment falls away more easily than most. This is because, once you have earned entry to one of the scholar cities, you will find you have access to a total library — Borges was right about that — and can surround yourself in your chosen quarters with as many volumes as you like, including books you never got round to writing and publishing while you were still in a physical body."

He changed appearance again. He became the young Mircea, a wild young man who made many mistakes, chasing women, frequenting Romanian bordellos, flirting with the fascists of the Iron Guard. He did not regret going among women — he had life in him — but he felt bad about his early politics. He would not tell me what he had been made to watch on the screen of the Biograph. But a few still photographs passed from his mind to mine. They showed young Mircea's infatuation with the handsome young fascist leader they called the Captain; the bitter disappointment in the face of a Jewish friend; a pogrom in a country village; bodies piled in the back of an oxcart; men in green shirts marching in formation, making the shape of an arrow cross, at a mass funeral; a secret meeting with a German agent.

The rooster crowed again.

"There is something you can do for me." He indicated that if I came across some memento of the Iron Guard and could bury it on his account, he would be grateful. This would lighten his burden.

The rooster crowed for a third time. This was clearly the end of the conversation. "You should study Romanian folklore," he told me. "The country people say that the rooster is one of the few animals whose forms cannot be taken by evil spirits." His own spirits seemed to be reviving. There was mischief in his face as he shapeshifted again and showed himself, briefly, in the furs and armor of a medieval *voivod*. Then I was alone on the terrace, watching mist roll along the valley.

I collapsed onto my bed. When I closed my eyes, I found myself in front of an immense marble staircase. It rose between tall pillars, going up and up for several floors. At the stop was a familiar figure in a white uniform. I was amazed to recognize Joseph Stalin. He was striding around, giving orders. I saw his shadow darkening the land, turning the fields blood-red.

Was this one of Mircea's dreams? Had he sent it to me to help me understand why he had chosen the fascists in the 1930s and the Axis in the Second World War?

I'm on a train, going up into the mountains. Through the window, I see that the roofs of the houses are more and more steeply pitched. Above them, jagged peaks glow silver-white. I know this landscape. We may be near Sinaia, the resort town and former royal capital, on our way to the villa. In his early years, Mircea must have escaped here many times during sweltering Bucharest summers. Ah, we are pulling into a station. I expect to get out and discover what is going on here. Instead, the train passes the station and makes an odd loop. We are approaching a tunnel. There are words carved in the stone. They are not in English, but I understand them to mean:

Every important writer, like every mythology, offers a creation story. Writers are world makers.

It sounds like something Mircea might have written. Maybe I can ask him if we manage to talk again. To my surprise, I find that the train is going to the Oriental Institute of the University of Chicago. I did not know you could get there from here. But Mircea did. I feel sure he has shown me where to find him again.

Think of a library. What better place for book lovers to find each other? A library or a museum, which is a library of images and material culture. I suggested to the group that we were going to go to a place like this, where any kind of information can be found and a master teacher may prove to be available. We would use drumming, of course, to liberate our traveling selves, as shamans have done for millennia. I did not know whether Mircea experimented with shamanic drumming, but he was familiar with it as an archaic technique of ecstasy.

Any tree can be the One Tree. Any library or museum, in the imaginal realm, can be a portal to the Total Library, the Akashic Records, the infinite repository of nonlocal mind. Today, because of my dream, I was going to Chicago.

I look at the photo of Mircea walking in snow across a courtyard. He is wearing a beret and a dark heavy overcoat. He is an old man, but there seems to be some sparkle in his eyes. The photo was taken at the University of Chicago, where he held a chair in religious studies for many years. The Oriental Institute is nearby, and so is the office of the anthropologist who inspired the character Indiana Jones. Surely it can't be too hard to keep a date with Mircea here.

The photograph opens like a window, and I am in that courtyard, in light snow, but Mircea has vanished from the scene, because it is not where we agreed to meet. I make my way, through clumps of students bundled up against the snow, to the Oriental Institute. I am amazed that the custodian can see me. He asks me to check my bag. I wasn't aware that I was carrying a bag, but now I see that I have been hauling something as heavy as a suitcase, but cubical. I am curious to know what's in my baggage and sneak a look before I head toward my appointment. The bag is full of books. No surprise there. What does amaze me is that the books include typescripts of books I have written, ones left unfinished or unpublished. It seems I have been carrying the burden of leftovers I couldn't bring myself to leave behind, old drafts that become a paper prison when you try to get back inside them. I know already I won't be coming back for this bag when I am finished with Mircea.

I pass the lions on guard at the foot of the great marble stairs. They raise up and pad behind me. I walk straight ahead, toward the winged bulls of the Assyrian room. Mircea, in a sport coat, is waiting by the statue of a god with human features, the long, curled Assyrian beard, nested bull horns for a headdress, and an amazing robe. The carved stone streams like water all down his body. It falls from his shoulders like a cascade of water. In the stream fish are swimming and leaping. It all comes alive as I look.

"I have dreams where I become aware I am dreaming because fish are swimming in midair."

Mircea does not dignify this with a direct response. "I thought you would know him," he gestures toward the statue. "This is Nabu, patron of writers, giver of knowledge, keeper of the archive baskets of the gods. From a civilization where you have a prehistory. Look at him more closely."

I do as I am told. I see that Nabu is holding a vessel from which four jets of water are streaming. Two jets spray over his shoulders and flow down his back. Two splash down the front of his garment to his feet. The ultimate Flow God. Perhaps the perfect guardian for a conversation between writers, though I do have a soft spot for muses.

"I've been thinking about men and women," Mircea announces. "Another of my regrets is that although I loved women and often gave them pleasure, I can't say that I ever understood them. This is also your condition."

He walks toward one of the winged bulls. "You have a Mesopotamian connection. You knew this when you were very young, though humans are forgetful animals. If I were you, I would take a story from that milieu and use it as a mirror for my own life and my own time."

"What story are you talking about?"

"The greatest one, of course. The descent of Inanna. The mystery of how and why the Queen of Earth and Heaven decides to go down to the netherworld to be hung on a meat hook."

"I know many women who identify with that story. There are women's groups that base rituals on it."

"Can you say that you understand it?"

"To be honest, not entirely."

He snorts. "You're a man! You may never understand it. But you can enter the story and write it as what you are, a man who knows women in the biblical sense and yet may not know them at all."

I am now very uncomfortable, because I remember enough of the story of Inanna to guess where this is going.

When Inanna goes down to the underworld, her consort, Dumuzi, forgets all about her. When she comes back to the sunlit world, she is enraged to discover that he has been having a fine old time without her. She calls on the terrible *galla* demons to drag him down to the underworld so he can experience what she has been through. Dumuzi dreams that the demons are coming for him and tries every way to escape, but even with the help of his sister, he can't elude the wrath of the goddess.

"Write the story of the descent of Dumuzi. Show us how a man can be transformed when he is made to endure everything that men have done to women. Bring him back worthy to be a consort for the Goddess. Have him risk everything to win her back."

I am moved, even to tears. "You have gone through this."

He does not respond. I wonder how many tests he has faced and how many worlds he has made or unmade since he left this one.

He reminds me that he has asked a small favor, easier to

execute than the rehab of a Sumerian god. I ask Lucian to help me find what is needed before our fire ceremony toward the end of the retreat.

Our firekeepers had done well. The logs were placed upright, leaning against each other, making the form of a tepee or a rustic pyramid. The kindling welcomed the flame, and soon the whole construction was blazing. I asked the spirits of earth and wind and fire for their blessing, promising that what we released would feed them. I offered tobacco and *pálinka* for the ancestors, and asked for their blessing too.

In this country of bears, we sang the bear song in the local language.

> *Nu plange micutule, nu plange micutule*
> *Ursul danseaze pentru tine, ursul danseaze pentru tine*
> Don't cry little one, don't cry little one
> The bear is coming to dance for you, the bear is coming to
>   dance for you

One by one, we advanced to the fire and gave it the things we had written or crafted, representing what we meant to release from our lives and our energy fields. Each time we consigned an object to the fire, we blew into the flames, because spirit travels on the breath. The operation brought tears to many. Someone releasing shame and grief vomited into the fire. This was relieved by wild laughter when a woman with raven hair burned a stick man, anatomically detailed and correct, representing an old lover.

It took me longer than most to do my own releasing. I burned the typescript of an old book a few pages at a time, taking care that the fire did not reject me by blowing it back. I knew I must do this after my encounter with the guard at the Oriental Institute.

The book might rise again from the flames, but first its old self had to be erased. I added the contents of a bottle of cognac, my favorite spirit that can be contained in this way, because I recognized that spirit of one kind may inhibit spirit of another.

It was not yet done. I took from my pocket the green flag that Lucian had found for me. I was amazed that he had been able to disinter this relic of a notorious fascist movement. "I told you I know the people of this area very well," was all he would say after he had made a trip to a nearby village when I confided my need to do something for Mircea.

When I unfolded the flag, the barred cross looked like the bars of a jail cell. Amazing that any political party, let alone a fascist one — fascists are usually better at calling up the glamour of the Dark Side — would have made this their emblem. It was the symbol of the Legion of the Archangel Michael, better known as the Iron Guard, which once captured Mircea's imagination. He had not pulled triggers or denounced his former Jewish friends publicly, but he knew he was complicit in the crimes of this movement, and he had not yet found it possible to absolve himself completely, even sitting up there in the pose of an ascended master.

"On behalf of our beloved professor, I release a history of guilt and infamy. May he be forever free of the prison of memory, able to teach and inspire new generations, and to choose his next life in perfect clarity."

The prison bars were seized by the flame. The fire leaped up wildly.

The dogs were barking, shaking the wire fences of their kennels. People gasped and shouted. Was the spectacle so moving? Lucian yelled at me to look between the trees. I saw a great brown bear, standing. There were more bears behind it, also up on their hind legs, swaying and dancing. This was not possible. These must be the Gypsy dancers in bear costumes you saw in this country at festival time. Lucian grabbed my arm, drawing me away as the bears came from the trees and danced around the fire. Surely they were looking for food scraps. Some of the women had brought candy and cookies, to release sugar from their bodies — and to snack on later.

Ursul danseaze pentru tine

The words swelled from within me, and soon all of us were singing. The dogs fell silent. No harm would come to us here.

"The bear has come to dance for you," I said softly to the man whose mind I had been in. "The prison bars cannot hold you now. Go in freedom into the clear light, or where your spirit calls you."

Dreamtakers

Your night dreams are an essential corrective to the delusions of the day. They hold up a mirror to your everyday actions and attitudes, and put you in touch with deeper sources of knowing than the everyday mind. Lose your dreams, and you may lose your inner compass. You may even lose your world.

1

I have been suffering from a dream drought for weeks. Each morning, I wake listless, my head foggy, disinclined to rise from my bed, even though the cold slush and drizzle of our protracted winter has turned overnight into glorious summer sunlight. On drab days, I have often turned to my dreams for excitement and solace. Faced with the perennial writer's challenge of covering the blank page, I have gone to my dreams for images so fresh and compelling that they brought my wordsmith willingly into play in order to craft language to hold them. Now I cannot bear even to open the scuffed green leather covers of my journal without fresh words to greet the day.

I stumble out into the street to walk the dog, carrying a couple of shirts for the laundry. The people around me seem dozy or programmed, pulled by their own dogs or their workday schedules, marching toward the towers of the state office complex or the dappled greens of the park. A stray picker with a few soda cans in his shopping cart tells me my dog is cute. A kid double-parks, hurling volleys of rap music at late sleepers in the houses. A blowsy blonde woman carries armfuls of roses into the florist's store on the corner. The store windows shake as workmen punch holes in the sidewalk with pneumatic drills. I search face after face. Have these morning people dreamed? Of course they have dreamed. We all dream, don't we? Even sleeping rats dream; it shows up in their brainwaves. I read that in a magazine. I want to ask the people around me, "What did you dream?"

I try the question on the girl in the dry cleaner's. She has a nose ring and a Grateful Dead T-shirt.

"My dreams are kinda weird," the Deadhead girl tells me. "But I don't remember from last night. I gotta get up too early to work."

Karen Vanderzee is in the park, elegant and equine in tailored slacks, walking her full-size poodle. I wait diplomatically until she has used a plastic bag and disposed of it in one of the bins before I try my question on her.

"I dreamed my ex was cheating on me with my best friend," she tells me, her eyes unreadable behind her dark glasses. "And I found out that was true. But that was before my divorce. I don't dream anymore."

Milt is sitting on a bench near the fountain, admiring the flower beds or the girl volunteers who are tending them. Milt is in his eighties and is the park philosopher.

"What's to dream?" he replies to my question. "Life is good. Enjoy the day."

He may have a point, I concede, as I watch a harem of brown-headed ducks following a green-headed duck across the pond. Wally splashes out into the water after a stick that I throw for him. Wally never gets tired of chasing a stick, or getting wet. I stop when my arm gets weary.

Back at the house, I call my mother. She tells me she doesn't dream anymore. Maybe it's the medication. She is crying when she tells me she never dreamed of my father after the heart attack that killed him.

I return my agent's call about the Chinese-language rights to my last book. He says he always has the same dream. He dreams he is faxing a knish to his brother in Los Angeles.

I walk round the block to Eleanor's Hair-Em to have a trim. Eleanor is usually a reliable fountain of dreams. I borrowed one of her dreams — a remarkably detailed and lurid drama in which she was in the body of an aging Hollywood sex siren receiving a series of lovers in an opulent hotel suite — for a TV script.

But as she pushes my head back into the sink for a rinse, Eleanor confesses that she too is going through a dry spell in her dream life. Could be the waning moon.

Eleanor's next client, a voluble lady called Rosa, flops down on the sofa and jumps right in. "I dream all the time, and in color!" From then until Eleanor shows me my weathered profile in a hand mirror, Rosa speaks without pause, sharing her dream flow from the previous night. "Jerry comes into the salon and a guy who looks like The Rock is leading him on a leash, and this cop who looks like my uncle Ben wants to ticket everybody, and Paula — that's my ex's ex — is dropping black jellybeans through a mail drop in my door (except I don't have a mail drop in my door), and I have to go to the bathroom real bad but I can't get in because my mom has left a pile of diapers in the doorway…" and on and on, until I am listing in the chair, ready to fall and lie, stupefied, on the linoleum floor, with my severed hairs drifting up my nose.

As I flee the salon, it strikes me that if my dreams were like Rosa's, I would not miss them much. This makes me realize that the dream drought I'm suffering is not absolute. Most mornings, I wake with *something* — a flimsy, fading image, usually quite dull and drab, not worth holding. Something has stayed with me today. What was it? Taking three plastic bags, instead of the usual two, on Wally's morning walk. How exhilarating and transcending! A mixed review for something I had written. Boring and depressing, not something I wanted to retain.

I call Melissa, the sister I never had, at her office and ask her to meet me for lunch at Camilo's. The margaritas are okay, and the hot sauce is hot.

Melissa does not look so good. She's pale, with black rings around her eyes. She says she has not been sleeping well.

"Dreams?"

She shakes her head. "I haven't remembered a dream in weeks."

"That's my problem too. I feel like I'm missing the movies."

"Could be the weather. I get migraines when the weather changes."

"I never noticed that weather affected my dream recall."

"What's the last dream you remember?"

"Oh, I don't know. I remember *something* most days. It's just like somebody got all the good stuff and left me with the junk mail. Last night I dreamed how many poop bags I would need for Wally on his morning walk. I haven't remembered a juicy dream in a long time."

"It's funny." Melissa licks salt from her lips. "It's not just you and me. My best friend at work — the one I share dreams with all the time — is going through a dream drought too. And this new receptionist, who thought we were weird for talking about dreams, is suddenly sharing all this stuff from her own dreams. But it's so garbled and boring everyone starts running out of the room."

"I experienced something like that today." I tell her about Rosa's verbal diarrhea in the hair salon.

"I wish there was something we could do. You know, like take a pill. They give us pills to make us go to sleep. There ought to be a dream pill."

"Maybe there is." I have a bright idea. "Close your eyes and open your hand."

I open a little round tin I happen to have in my pocket, take out two lemon drops, and place them on Melissa's palm with ritual care.

"Dream pills."

"They're lemon drops."

"They're whatever you want them to be. When you wake up tomorrow, if you don't remember a dream, put one on your tongue and let it dissolve. By the time the dream pill has dissolved, you'll be right inside the dream space."

The sour lemon drops remind me of the lemons I used to eat when I was a kid, cut into slices and dipped in the sugar bowl. As I let one dissolve on my tongue, walking back to the house, I find myself traveling across the years, back inside a scene of my child-hood. If a lemon drop can take me through time, why shouldn't it take us back into a forgotten dream?

As I surface groggily into another day, the only legacy from the night is a low-grade headache. I groan when my daughter comes in to kiss me on her way to the school bus, and groan again when my wife kisses me on her way to the office. I am more fatigued than when I went to bed. More than fatigued, I feel drained. I abandon my writing quota for the morning, close the shutters against the morning sunlight, and fall back into bed.

I'm sick; that's obvious. Can lack of dreaming make you sick? I think about writers who get sick when they are about to produce their best work, or deliver their best in the midst of illness. Patrick White had to get very ill before he started writing his best. I picture Robert Louis Stevenson, writing in bed in a freezing cabin on Saranac Lake, gasping and hacking as he puffed his eternal cigarette. But RLS dreamed profusely, especially when he was sick. He said his brownies came to him in his dreams and helped him do his best work. Where are my dreams, and my brownies?

I lie on one side, then the other. I lie on my back. I pull the sheet up over my head, as I used to do when I was a boy, to make a tent of adventure. Nothing helps. My inner screen is blank. My mind is a mess of petty thoughts and routine concerns. I feel cheated. A great door has been closed in my face, and I can't even see where it used to be.

I remember my silly, childish game with Melissa and the lemon drops. What do I have to lose? I find the tin and place one of the lemon drops on my tongue, wondering whether Melissa actually followed my instructions. Now the phone is ringing in the alcove. I hear my own voice on the tape, then a woman's voice that might be Melissa's, except it's a little too sharp and strident for her. I let that go. I bite down on the last fragment of the candy, releasing a sharp flow of juice that trickles down my throat.

The scene behind my eyelids is no longer altogether dark and formless. Something hangs there, like a net. I attempt to change the image. I open and close my eyes. The net is still there. I fumble in my wife's dresser for her black silk scarf and wind it tight around my eyes. The net is still there. I try to go round it, but it surrounds me on all sides. I try to get through the mesh, but that doesn't work. I get the nasty feeling that this isn't simply a net, but a web.

Yes, it's a web, rather sticky to the touch. As soon as I touch it, I regret my action. I have the sense that I have drawn the attention of something very unpleasant and that it is moving toward me very fast.

This is *real*, my senses are screaming.

The phone rings again. Melissa's voice comes over the machine.

I reach for the phone before she hangs up. I have the creepy feeling that when I opened my eyes, I left some part of me behind, in the web.

"Did you do it?" Melissa sounds scared.

"Do what?"

"The dream pill thing. Did you go back in?"

"I tried."

"Did you see it?"

"All I saw was something like a net. I couldn't get out."

"Me too." She sounds choked. "It's not right. It shouldn't be there. Can we do something?"

"I don't know."

"Do you think it's some kind of illness? I mean, is it just us, or do other people have this?"

"I don't know."

"Listen, I've got to get to the office. Will you call me later?"

"Sure."

I fall back on the bed. This time, I get nothing when I close my eyes. Just blackness shifting into blurry grays as light grows stronger in the bedroom.

I get dressed, feeling limp and listless. My feet drag as Wally pulls me toward the park. It's another beautiful day, but I do not trust the color and movement around me.

You're starting to remember.

I wheel around. The voice is so close I expect to find someone right behind me. The picker is there, with his shopping cart filled with soda cans and beer bottles.

"Did you say something?"

"Got any empties?"

This is going to be another lost day. Back home, I turn on the computer, but waste my time on email instead of working on an overdue article. Before noon, I am playing solitaire with the computer and drinking my first glass of wine.

I grab a microwave dinner and put on the news channel. The lead stories are the same. Tweetstorms and corruption scandals. High-school kids gunned down by a crazy loner with an automatic rifle he should never have been allowed to possess. Smug men in government denying the evidence of global warming, pushing for drilling and logging on our last wilderness preserves.

Do these people dream?

I drink enough by early afternoon to feel ready for a nap. As I throw myself down on the bed, I will myself to dream and remember.

Dream and remember.

When I was sick as a boy, I developed the trick of lying quite still, on my back, and letting myself float up until — with a twist and a turn — I was looking down at my body on the bed. I did not have a name for the part of me that could get out of the body this way. I just knew that it could.

I am lying on my back now, focused on the sense of letting myself float up above my body. I see a sleeping figure, lying in something like a hammock. The sleeper is very familiar. I study the webbing. It extends in all directions. Not a hammock, but a net or web of immense size. Things are moving beyond the web, flying at it, trying to get through. Only a few of them make it through the mesh. These are dull, flimsy things that remind me of bulk-mail envelopes.

Beyond the net, there is the flash of bright colors and gauzy wings. There are lovely, luminous things out there. Are these the dreams I've been missing?

When they come close, the net ripples and snatches at them. One of the beautiful winged creatures is caught, its wings bound in sticky threads, like a spider's lunch.

I thought of the dreamcatcher my daughter made for me in a school project. In the Native way, as I understand it, a dreamcatcher is meant to catch bad dreams and let only the good ones through. I am looking at a horrible travesty of a dreamcatcher, a device that keeps out beautiful dreams and lets only junk mail through.

Someone, or something, has been playing a terrible joke on me. My rage boils up, and I tear at the fabric of the net, trying to open it up. As if in a dream, my anger gives me fingers like talons. I rip at the mesh, but it is withdrawn — pulled away at amazing speed.

How can this be happening? In the grainy dark, I see something like a giant sea spider, reeling and recoiling on many dark legs. Its full shape is concealed from me as it burrows backwards into a funnellike opening, pulling the web in with it.

I want to go into that funnel, and release the captive dream, but I do not relish the prospect of grappling with an arachnid bigger than myself in a confined space.

Sgardis. I know — without knowing the source of the information — that this is a name for the thing that has hidden itself inside the funnel.

My vision clears and widens. Released from the net, I have left my bedroom behind and am moving across the astral sea. Below me, around me, immense vistas open out. I see millions upon millions of sleepers suspended in the sea of dreams. Some have been targeted and masked, as I was, by personalized dream takers. Many, many more are drifting inside webs that now resemble vast industrial dragnets.

How did this happen?

What does it mean for humanity if people are deprived of their dreams?

A beautiful shimmering creature is winging toward me. It looks something like a manta ray and something like a morpho butterfly, but the face and torso are those of a lovely girl.

Her voice is bell music, forming words in my mind.

Come and we will show you.

2

I landed so hard I thought I had broken the bed. The image came to me of David Bowie hitting the ground in an old movie, *The Man Who Fell to Earth*. I needed to go to the bathroom, and put my feet on the floor, resigned to the fact that, yet again, I had no dreams. But wait. I had something. The memory of a being with celestial blue wings, like a giant morpho butterfly, and of something horrible and sticky, like a huge black spider web where people were trapped and drained of their vital juice.

Come and we will show you.

Had the morpho really spoken these words to me?

How could I possibly act on them?

You came part of the way. You found a hole in the sky. Follow the path you are starting to make for others.

My bathroom trip could wait. I lay flat on my back. I let myself rise from my body.

Don't lose it again, an inner voice told me. What was speaking was a wiser self. I cannot say whether it was a part of me or the voice of the blue butterfly.

As I rose from the body on the bed in a second body, I reached to my solar plexus and felt the subtle cord, smooth as silk but tough as fishing line, that tethered me to the physical. I would remember to follow the cord back, not to leave my body bereft of the Traveler again.

I focused my intention: find the blue butterfly.

I was going up, very fast. I shot up through the roof of the house. The city around me fell away. I was buffeted by strange, swirling winds that knocked me sideways, and tossed me, and had me plummeting down toward the park. I managed to break my fall before I crashed into the old weeping beech where kids hide themselves to neck and drink beer.

The thought of beer sent me through the open door of a tavern where Happy Hour was in full swing. I was welcomed loudly and warmly. The bartender set up a boilermaker for me — a beer with a shot — unasked. "On the house," he said. The crowd made room for me at the bar. From the next stool, a woman with the reddest lips I had ever seen leaned into me, inhaling the smell of my drink and my skin.

"Mmmm, what are you wearing?"

"Just myself."

She laughed and pressed against me. "I want you now," she breathed. "And you want me. I am beautiful. All men desire me." In that moment, I believed her. She was gorgeous and magnetic. Her touch was electric. She was willing me to take her, or be taken by her. But the avid faces looking at us unnerved me, making me feel that a spotlight had been turned on us in the murky twilight of the saloon.

I pulled away, and she hissed. Others were growling and hissing too. It came to me that they were all dead drunks, that a passing thought of beer had brought me to a Happy Hour of the Dead, and then to a sex trap. I willed myself out of the place, evading some barflies who tried to block me. I looked back, and corrected my impression that everyone here was dead. There were people slumped or frozen at the bar, or among the tables, that I recognized. Jerry was there. He lived in the next block. He had told me that morning — or some morning, I was losing track of days — that he never dreamed. I could see why. His dream soul, his traveling self, wasn't in his body, even on a part-time basis. It was living here, with the dead drunks.

I came out of the bar into deep fog. The ground beneath me was slippery, more mud than concrete or asphalt. The fog was inside me too, as if I had swallowed a few boilermakers. I recalled my intention, and spoke it aloud: find the blue butterfly.

A bird screamed above me. I looked up and saw an enormous red-tailed hawk hovering just overhead, squalling at me in a language I could not understand, but whose urgency was unmistakable. I began to lift off, as if it had seized me with its talons. Under the wings of the hawk, I rose through cloud banks and barriers that stretched like membranes to let me through. I came to a world that seemed crazy to me. Things rushed away at impossible angles. Staircases rose and ended in midair, or at a blank wall, or swung back and forth.

The beings of this world did not have solid form. They shape-shifted at bewildering speed. They looked like foxes and like saucepans, like grasshoppers and cascades of water. I learned they were masters of words and of breath.

They sang over me. They breathed strength and healing into me.

They told me, "We do this to open your ears, so you may hear clearly."

They put something in my eyes that stung like ginger, like hot chili sauce. They sang, "We do this to open your eyes and cleanse your perception."

The crazy world began to settle into form. The word masters now looked almost human, but golden, and winged.

They opened my mouth and breathed on my tongue. "We do this to open your mouth so you can speak the language of birds and peoples of all tribes can understand you."

Now birds and animals came to me in great numbers, and I saw that they were my friends. They said, "We will show you why humans have lost their dreams."

They showed me places where dream souls are held captive. Some have been stolen and serve murky agendas. Some got lost through bad habits and addictions, stuck in scenes like the Happy Hour of the Dead. Some are living in fake worlds. Many are caught in sticky webs, like bugs in a spider web. Some went missing because of trauma and grief and are actually being held safe — sometimes by animal families, sometimes by elders. It was hard for me to understand what I could do to help.

I was told, "You are going to ascend to a higher level." Traveling through mists or cloud banks, I entered the most beautiful landscape I had ever seen — a shining blue lake that glowed with electric fire. I had traveled so far. I was exhausted and saddened by what I had seen of the state of the dream souls. I let myself slip into the healing waters of the blue lake. Above me I saw the celestial blue butterfly. It had a lovely human face and the suggestion of a slender girl's body. It brought me blue water of life. I felt this coursing through my body, renewing, healing, restoring. I relaxed in the blue waters. Something streamed through the waters like an electric eel. It touched me and I felt lightning struck.

I was told, "The time of your death is now." I was not afraid. I rose from the body in the blue lake. I felt incredibly light and free.

I ascended in a body of light, to meet beings I knew to be

my guides on the highest level accessible to me in this time. They shone like the sun. I saw them as gods until my senses were changed again, and I realized that I was *home*. I had returned to the world of my home star. The gods were familiar, my soul kin. They infused me with memory of my soul purpose. They confirmed that I had been living in a world that has fallen into dark times because people have lost their dream souls, and thereby their connection with the higher worlds where we find the origin and purpose of our lives.

"I want to stay with you," I told them. "This is my home."

"We don't need you. People on Earth need you."

They made me look down from this height at the state of Earth. I felt nauseous. It was like looking down an incredibly tall elevator shaft. Across the distance, I could now see more of the state of humans. I saw people living like pigs, wallowing in muck, always hungry, stuffing themselves, jostling each other for more space at the feeding trough. I saw people living like snakes, having sex in indiscriminate heaps. I saw people who are slaves of a Dark Lord of Chaos, broken-willed, doing his bidding.

"I don't want to go back there."

"You agreed to do this work before you left us. You were given the chance to reconsider. You forgot your soul purpose because you succumbed to the miasmic conditions of the Cloaked Planet. You even lost your dream soul for a while. Now your memory is restored, you know you must go back. But you must go armed."

I found myself in an armory, an armory of soul. I was invited to choose my weapons. There were things here that might have come from the den of an ancient sorcerer — a rattle, a drum, a bone flute. There were stones and crystals, hollow bones, mirrors. Some of the tools were quite mysterious: a tuft of wool, part of an antler, fluff from a cattail, a small pumpkin.

I was drawn to an array of amber in many colors, from white to deep blue and black, and across the whole spectrum of yellow and orange. My choice was approved. I was shown how to use light amber to heal and conduct soul energy, and how to use dark amber to cleanse and protect. I left with dark amber in my left hand and bright amber in my right.

I returned to the blue lake. I reentered the body I had left bobbing in the water. I opened the eyes of my dream body. I found the silver cord that joined it to the body I left in my bedroom. I tugged gently on the cord and found myself flying down, very fast, with the amber in my hands.

I rose from my bed, remembering all of my journey. Now I could let myself pad to the bathroom and take a leak. I had aches throughout my body and a dry mouth, as if I had just come back jet-lagged from an intercontinental flight.

I looked at the clock. How long did I spend on the journey to the Blue Lake and the Star People? Less than two hours of tick-tock time.

I sat down with my journal and wrote fast, determined to get down every detail. I made little sketches that started to look like a shaman's map, the kind I had seen painted on skins and on birch bark.

I had work to do in the world. Where to begin? I pulled a Tarot card from a deck and got the Eight of Disks, sometimes called Prudence. My own name for it is Step by Step.

My dog had been very patient with me, but now he was urgent for his first walk of the day. I dressed and clipped on his leash. He ran ahead of me up the sidewalk toward the park.

In the next block Jerry waved at me from his stoop. I remembered that I had seen him during the night, in the Happy Hour of the Dead. I could smell beer on his breath.

"What's going on?"

I told him, "I've been doing some dreaming."

Worry lines creased his forehead. "Say what?"

"I said I've been dreaming."

Jerry scratched his head. "I don't know what that is." He brightened when he added, "Unless you mean watching dirty movies."

I shrugged and followed my dog up the street. Then it hit me that I had identified my first case. In the night I would seek Jerry's dream soul where I saw it before, in the Happy Hour of the Dead. I would do whatever it took to get him out of the bar. I would catch Jerry's dream soul like a fly in amber and take it on an excursion to restore his sense of meaning and his memory of soul family and soul purpose. I would blow his dream soul back into his body and watch over him as he opened his eyes in the morning, to ensure that they were reunited.

Step by step, one soul at a time. Tomorrow I would check whether he remembered what dreaming is.

My cell phone chimed. I swiped the screen to let the call through. Melissa said, "Hey, I dreamed again and it was about you. I saw you inside an amber egg, with a blue butterfly. Does that mean anything to you?"

"It means the world to me."

The Ride to Tethys

There is a House of Healing in the imaginal realm. As in the ancient temples of dream healing, the price of admission is the right dream. If what you grow from that dream in your imagination is big enough, you may invite another person who is in need to share in its power and healing, if they dare.

I have walked this path before, in many lives. It winds along a headland, with cliffs to my right that fall sheer to the ocean, which is turbulent today. The bees brought me here first, swarming around my dormant body to carry my traveling self to this place of healing and savage initiation. In all lives, death is the price of initiation. You die in order to be reborn.

I don't know what body I am in now, and I don't remember how I came here. My senses are all vividly alive. I am oppressed by stomach cramps and shooting pains in my legs that feel like electrical circuits misfiring. At the same time, I am drinking salt air. I welcome wind and sun on my face and lick my chapped lips.

I see figures ahead of me on the path. They are wearing simple garments, tunics and shifts, and sandals with many straps. Some lean on each other, or on sticks. I know that their sacks contain offerings to the gods of this place: oil for the lamps, honey cakes for the serpents, leftovers for the dogs, images of the body parts and internal organs the supplicants wish to have healed. They have come great distances, some of them, braving many perils, to a place where prayer has been valid and statues step off their pedestals in the night.

I look down, trying to see who I am. This man's body is hairier and has more olive oil in the skin than my usual one. I am wearing sandals like the others, and a simple pleated garment. I look ahead and see one of the pilgrims wrestling with something he is trying to remove from his sack. It squeals and shits in his arms. It is a little pink pig. I have seen this before too. To enter the House of Healing, you must be cleansed. One of the quickest ways to get bad stuff, heavy stuff — the things that bring disease and madness and addiction — out of your energy field is to put them into another living creature. Chickens are popular for this in many traditions. A pig, even a very young one, is a larger investment, suggesting that a more extensive cleanup is required. Even Christians know about this. Yeshua the exorcist used the Gadarene swine as others had done for centuries.

The pilgrim ahead of me has a better grip on his piglet now. He's throwing it like a medicine ball, out over the cliff. It screams as it hurtles down into the salt waves. My stomach churns. It feels as if something wants to burst from inside me.

I leave the path and walk the very edge of the cliff. I am seized by the form of vertigo that usually keeps me away from edges of this kind. I want to throw myself down. I have had to wrestle with myself to resist this pull from the depths. I have felt it on paths in the high Andes, by the open door of a train going over a bridge, even at the top of an escalator in a shopping mall. The waves surge and crash below me. I tell myself I am now permitted to let myself fall. All I have to offer now is myself.

I lean forward until my heels leave the earth. It is amazing how long I seem to hang in the air, as if time is frozen. Then I am shocked by the chill of the water. I want to be cleansed in this sea, whatever happens to the body I am using. The stomach pains return, more violent. I clutch at myself and realize I am holding something. It is shaped like a rough cube, and it is sloppy and flabby, like a chunk of raw pork. It is alive and squirming like that piglet. Can this have come from inside me? Where else?

I am gripped by the wild hope that if I can get this thing off me, I will be cleansed and released from the guilt and pain I have been carrying. The pork squirms and writhes in my arms. I struggle to get it off me. Then I see that something from the deep is taking an interest. A great eye rises like a drowned moon. Huge tentacles and pincers wave and sway. The giant beaklike mouth opens, while multiple limbs flail behind. I am facing my worst nightmare from boyhood, the giant squid that terrified me in the old movie of *Twenty Thousand Leagues under the Sea*. I make another, now desperate, attempt to release the raw pork. The kraken swallows it like an appetizer. Now it is coming for me.

Flight is impossible. Yet I discover I have other options. Round my wrists, unnoticed until now, are coils of gold wire. I flick my arms, and the wires lasso the sea monster's beak, preventing it from devouring me. With the hero's body I now inhabit, I can haul myself up onto its back. A fish spear is in my hand. I plunge the trident into the base of the monster's cranium. I can use this as a joystick to direct the beast toward where I need to go. I know my direction is toward deeper healing.

Tethys. It is not the name I want to hear, but it states my direction exactly.

We plunge deep, as deep as the realm of an oceanic power,

feminine but in no way human. Her name is Tethys. She is older than the gods of Olympus, and even Poseidon was scared of her. Her form is even more monstrous than that of the cosmic squid. There are openings in her body above and below. The mouth above is like that of a baleen whale, filled with a kind of rolling grid, through which she inhales life of all kinds, endlessly devouring, blowing back unwanted water. The aperture below — a place of birthing — looks similar, but works differently.

I make my choice. I swim through this unlikely vagina, leaving the kraken behind. I am rushed through submarine tunnels until at last I come to a vast pool teeming with life. The scene reminds me of a fish hatchery, and also the spawning of salmon. In this space, I feel myself refilling with vital energy and sexual power. I am gifted with the twin powers of primal sexuality and creation.

Nothing in excess, a voice reminds me, *was never your motto*.

I rise from the animal skin on the floor of the incubation chamber. I am charged with superabundant energy. I feel ridiculously, blazingly well. My body has returned to human proportions, but my skin is clear and golden, and I feel the aegis of the hero who mastered the cosmic squid in my energy field.

I am in the sacred dormitory of the House of Healing. I don't know how I got here from the womb of Ocean, but I am confident I have paid the price of admission. You come here only by invitation. You earn your invitation by bringing the right dream to the therapeuts, the priests and priestesses of the temple. I have been through this so many times, as supplicant and as priest. Did my ride to Tethys begin on the cliff, or here in the place of sacred dreaming? Does it matter? Here we don't ask, *Is it real?* We judge by results, not ontology.

The priestesses bathe and oil me and smirk when they see

how ready I am for female company. When they escort me to the Throne of Memory, a capering jester waves a fake penis longer than a monkey's tail at the women and me.

The Throne of Memory stands above a stage, an apron of stone in a theater with many terraced rows of stone seats. I remember this too. Those who survive the sacred night and have received healing are required to deliver their stories before an audience. I must have received good advance reviews, because hundreds of people are gathering, together with the dogs. A pair of black dogs with high, pointy ears sniff me and seem to approve.

I tell my story and don't need to raise my voice for it to carry through the whole theater.

I leave out some details of what happened inside the ocean of Tethys.

Before I am done, the therapeuts are leading several people from the audience onto the stage in front of me. These are the ones most in need of the power of a bigger story than the ones they have been living, of a fresh myth to replace the old chronicles of failure and loss and despair. My task now is to make a gift of what I lived and survived — of the battle of a hero or heroine with a cosmic squid — to the receiver who can take it into mind and body and make best use of it.

I know my receiver even before she looks up, and I see the longing in her eyes. She reminds me of someone, a woman who has not yet found her way out of a black well of memories of abuse and shame. Wide-hipped, a little slack-bodied, the woman onstage is very like Karen.

I tell her, "You are going to be me, but at the end of the drama you are going to be more of yourself. You are going to fight a great battle. At the end of it, you will claim your full power, mastering and riding the Cosmic Squid." I have settled on this name for the monster now. "Are you willing to take this on?"

She is scared, but she says, "Yes. But how?"

Through theater, of course. It's what we do in the House of Healing whenever we have the right script.

There are volunteers eager to play all the roles in the drama. There is even keen competition to embody the horrible raw fatty pork. Human actors make pincers and tentacles and the great drowned moon. There is wild humor, breaking into belly laughs across the whole theater, as the quivering pork faces the pincers and the gobbling beak. There is wilder applause when the woman cast as heroine stands on top of a mound of humped bodies that have become the Cosmic Squid.

I feel something streaming from me to the heroine as a great shaft of light when she claims her power to tame and harness the beast and stands before us at center stage, shining bright. I am weary now. I have earned some rest.

I close my eyes. When I open them, the phone is ringing. I look at the bedside clock. It's only six in the morning. I don't take many phone calls, and this one is probably spam. I flip back the cover of my phone, intending to nix the call, but the number is familiar.

"Karen?"

"I waited as long as I could. I'm so excited. I have to tell you about this dream we were in."

I glug some water from the bottle I keep beside my bed — you really don't want to drink from containers you left open overnight — while Karen's words crash over themselves like waves rolling in.

"And you know what they called this sea monster I had to fight? They called it the Cosmic Squid. Isn't that great?"

"Very cool."

"But wait. It gets even better. While I was waiting to call you, I turned on the local public radio station. They were interviewing this composer and guitarist named Henry Kaiser. Then they played one of his tunes. Guess what it's called. 'Cosmic Squid'!"

"No way."

"Seriously. What do you make of that?"

"I think sometimes we get a nod or a wink from the world."

Then she says, "Whatever happened overnight, I found my joy again. I'm not going to keep on going back and back. Whenever I feel memories dragging me down, I can stand up. I can ride that freaking Cosmic Squid."

"Fantastic."

It did feel fantastic. But of course I had to check. We judge by results. I found that radio interview with Henry Kaiser. The track they played is called "Celestial Squid," not "Cosmic Squid." But that's near enough.

Flight Conditions

You are pretty sure you are dreaming, because you have this amazing body and are at least twenty years younger. Your skin may even be blue as a god's, or an avatar's. You are itching to fly. You have done so in other dreams, and loved the thrill of catching a thermal and riding high over the world. But pause for a moment before you jump off that cliff. Different worlds have different physics. The world you are dreaming in may be no less solid than the one where you left your regular body, and the body you are in may be just as breakable.

The forest is green fire, bursting and thrusting with life. Below the great tree where I am stretched out, the slope of the mountain drops in green splendor for miles, down to a river that from this height is green and small as a grass snake. A bright green vine as thick as my wrist bends in a loop between me and the sky.

My attention shivers. My cheek is on a pillow. My awareness is back in the body I left here, on the bed. Gray morning light comes through a narrow gap in the curtains above the bed. I smell bacon, and my inner dog is ready to go downstairs. But the tug of the green world is deeper.

I plunge back into that world. My body feels stronger and lighter, perfectly toned. I want to jump off the cliff and fly. I have done this so many times before, in other dreams. I will my wings to sprout from my shoulders again. This seems less successful than usual. While my body in the green world feels entirely physical, my wings seem flimsy and insubstantial, hardly more than a notion. This does not matter, surely. When I take the jump, I'll find myself flying. Flying in dreams is easy. All you have to do is fall, and fail to hit bottom.

I am at the very edge of the precipice. My toes curl over the edge. I notice these toes are much longer than my regular toes, and can curl into a loop, like my regular fingers. Cool. What else can this body do?

I consider a diver's stance, then spread my arms and start gently flapping.

Stop, says an inner voice, a voice I have learned to listen to. *Look at who you are.*

I pull back. Now I am outside and above the person at the edge of the cliff. I see him back away from the edge. He is puzzled. He sniffs the air, searching for something he senses but cannot see.

Another hand reaches for him. There is a lovely woman under the tree, the slopes of her body arranged in such abandon that I feel sure the two of them must have been making love before I interrupted. "Woman" is not quite right. They resemble humans, but they are much taller, with those prehensile feet. The male has little horns among his long dark hair. Not horns, exactly. The nubs of antlers. His tawny body is covered with fine, light, silky hair. Something sways behind him as he returns to the embrace of the female. Is it a tail?

I am no longer observing. I am with him, in him, in his ritual of mating. He seems to be alone with his mate, yet I have no doubt this is a ritual, more than sex, more even than the love-making of two individuals. As he plunges deep in her body, I feel energy streaming from the roots of the great tree. And something more joins him — us — surging in at the base of the spine. The dragon is on him, and in us.

Now we can fly, I tell myself.

Again I hear the caution of an inner guide. This deer-man's body is strong, and it can perform acrobatics beyond the human range. He can swing down the mountain face on vines, and leap from branch to branch. He can ride a thing like a dragon, the thing with which he is now bonded in another way. But he cannot fly. If I jumped this body over the precipice, it would probably be broken and destroyed on the rocks far below.

I thought that in dreaming, people can fly, because we go outside the physical body and are no longer confined by the laws of physical reality. This is often true. But when we travel in these ways, we are not necessarily disembodied. We travel in a subtle energy body, often called the *astral body* or the *dream body*. And we can take on other bodies.

Dreaming, we not only change states of consciousness, we switch worlds, stepping from one reality into another one. The other worlds may be quite as substantial as the one in which we stub our toes or spill coffee. They have their own laws of physics, and what we do with the bodies we are using can have physical consequences — not only in these other worlds, but on the bodies we left dormant when we took off on our adventures.

There are worlds in which you can ride a dragon, but can't fly by yourself. Before you jump off a cliff, make sure you are in a body that is capable of flight.

The Silent Lovers

Yeats said that the living can assist the imaginations of the dead. We may even be called on to play advocates for the dead as they go through their transitions on the way to choosing their next life experience. I did not know this until I found myself in a theater in the imaginal realm.

A single bed with an iron frame and an oatmeal-covered blanket. The bed has recently been used. The blanket is pulled back a little, revealing a furrowed sheet with a damp stain near the pillow. Nearby is a small wooden table and two chairs. In one of them sits a muscular young man with curly black hair, wearing a singlet and dark pants with suspenders hanging loose. In the other chair is a narrow-faced man in a gray business suit. He may be forty. He is reading a newspaper and smoking the one cigarette he allows himself at this time of day. The newspaper is large-format (not tabloid), and the front page has fewer photos and graphics than is typical today.

The time of day is important. It is early morning, around

dawn. This is the usual time for assignations between the man in the gray suit and his lover. After he has finished his cigarette, he will walk to his office in a law firm a few blocks away. The young man will go back to bed.

There is the smell of sex in the room, but hardly a hint of sensuality. Sex here is taken like a glass of water, as a necessary but passionless release. There are very few words between the gay lovers, and almost no physical gestures of affection. The younger man seems capable of strong emotion, and of physical violence, but he is more likely to speak with his fists than with words. The lawyer finishes reading his paper, places his stub in a tin ashtray, and rises to leave.

Why am I seeing this?

I shift my focus, trying to see more of the room. It is strangely empty. When I search the shadows beyond the reach of the bare bulb hanging at the center, I find that the room is completely empty, except for an enamel washbasin. No furnishings except for the single bed and the table and chairs. No clothes. The walls look insubstantial, like part of a stage setting, the kind of pasteboard screens that roll on wheels.

I pull back, taking a broader view. I am definitely watching something that is playing out onstage. I can see the curtains on either side of the scene. I look across rows of velvet-padded seats. There is just one person in the audience, a man with a narrow face in a gray suit. I look back at the stage. There is no doubt. The audience consists of the lawyer onstage. He is watching himself.

I now have information about him, an instant download from an unknown source. The lawyer's name is Kinsella. He lives with his mother in a brownstone in Brooklyn. She is mostly absent. When he is out, she sits at a window behind a lace curtain, talking to herself about things she sees that are not in the street. When he comes home in the evening, he makes her dinner and sometimes has to spoon her food into her mouth. There is no touching or talking. He has never forgiven her for failing to do anything when his father, drunk and raging like a red boar, beat him for crying and later for asking questions.

I know that this is why Kinsella cannot express emotion. The scene being played onstage presents his deepest regret, that he has lived an expressionless life.

I understand that he is undergoing a life review. He is being shown scenes from his life to help him get his story straight, to make sense of what he did and did not do, to recognize his deepest regrets. This is essential if he is to make the right decisions about where he will go next.

This means, of course, that Kinsella is dead. I look again at the curly-haired, muscular young man in the singlet. His name is Billy. I know now that his friends are waiting outside, in the street, for Kinsella to come down from this rented room and walk the few blocks to the law office, where he works on contracts and estate matters. They intend only to roll the queer for his money, but a careless blow and a fall will leave Kinsella dead on the sidewalk.

This happened decades ago, perhaps in the 1940s. I see the lunch counter that Kinsella will not visit on this day, where the cheerful blonde waitress in the red polka-dot dress brings him the same coffee and sandwich every day and gets a dime tip but never a smile.

I have the sense that Kinsella is not alone, after all, in this theater of the soul. There is a second figure beside and a little behind him. This must be his advocate, the attorney for the deceased. It is normal procedure for an advocate to be assigned to anyone undergoing the process of life review and preparation for what will follow.

I would like to study Kinsella's advocate, to learn what is

involved in this type of work and who is selected for it. But Kinsella's adviser is only a shadow.

I lean forward and realize that he is *my* shadow. This is astonishing. How can I be the advocate for a dead Irish-American lawyer of whom, until now, I knew nothing? Does this mean I am dead too?

I do not pursue these questions right away because I feel the urgency of my client's need.

The priests made me what I became.

He will not be looking for a priestly figure, and probably not for any figure from the pantheon of his church, to help him now. Does he fear damnation?

You have been in hell already, I seek to reassure him. *Hell is on Earth.*

He is weeping now. The shell has cracked.

I take him forward, to a different theater, this one more like a cinema, where he can review life options that may be before him when he has completed his process of cleansing and purgation and reeducation. I am scouting on his behalf.

We are agreed that he does not need privilege or money in his next life — money got him killed — but a chance to express his feelings, to give and receive love and joy, to dance and delight in the world of the senses. I am drawn to Bahia, to the wild color and music of Pelourinho, to a family that is very poor but rarely hungry, where many children are loved and allowed to play in freedom. Kinsella likes men more than women out of his former body as well as in it. So he will be Rosa Terezinha.

I feel an approving nod from a superior intelligence. I realize that I am being trained and tested for a role I can take on when I have left my present body behind. I knew that the living can assist the imaginations of the dead — as a dead poet insisted — but I am surprised that someone with a body on Earth can be authorized and enabled to play the role of advocate for the dead in the transits that lead to birth.

I am told, in a voice I have learned to trust, "In your present life, you are more active out of your body than in it. Remember you are not confined to a single body, or a single reality. You have been on our faculty, as both student and teacher, in many lifetimes. We gave you Kinsella to test your empathy. A man as cold and unfeeling, as void of color and drama as this, might not have engaged your fellow feeling in your present life. You must be willing to defend any case that is given to you. This time, you passed the test."

The Grand Duke
Calls My Name

A story is calling to me, through my window in a stone tower in a dry wood, near the medieval French town of St. Martin de Londres. I hear *sangliers* — wild boars — snaffling and snorting and muttering red secrets. I reach behind my back, to the place above my left kidney where a boar marked me in another country. The boar is part of an old, old story that snares me from time to time. I would prefer not to reenter that now.

A woman is laughing manically near the huge swimming pool, which was drained when the leaves started to fall. Her screech is enraging the boars and allows me little chance to sleep, even when I close the window and the door to my little balcony.

At last the woman goes to bed, or passes out, and the boars fall silent.

I drift on the bed, half in my body and half out of it.

Hours later, when the woods are silent under the Peak of the Sainted Wolf, a long cry reaches for me.

Hoooooooooo!

The cry is repeated, then veers into a popping, screeching, jabbing monologue. Somewhere in there, I hear my name.

The windows rattle, the bedside cabinet shakes, a door slams on the landing. The moody winds of the Midi are gusting wildly tonight.

Robert!

The cry is closer now, eerie yet seductive. My name is in there, no doubt of it. The accent is French: *Ro-bear!* In part of myself, I want to rise from my bed and fly out the window, to see what's up. Perhaps I can join the night owl and share its vision. Owl eyes have helped me in the dark before.

Some instinct of self-preservation restrains me. Who knows what it would take to get back to my body? The Traveler in me is ready for the assignment. I feel him expanding, stretching my energy field, threatening to slide out from my feet if I won't let him out from any other place. I am firm. I am not going to let my double leave the room. I need as much of me in the room as I can manage.

The owl that called my name is the *chouette*, or tawny owl. I know that in this corner of France, they call it the Grand Duc. I try to tame my situation by shaping a witticism: when you hear the owl call your name, it is a comfort to know that you got one at the top of the social register.

I don't find this funny enough. My sense of humor is languishing. This always means trouble. I don't want to leave any world — or come back to one — without my sense of humor.

With a deep sigh, I lie down on my back, nose pointed at the ceiling. This is the posture, and the time of night, when I find that inner guides become available. There is one voice I have come to trust beyond all others.

Before I have framed my request for guidance, the voice cuts through my mental chatter, cold and sharp as a chef's knife.

The time of your death is now.

I take a cold plunge. For a moment, I can't breathe. It is exactly like falling into water half my body temperature. I am lost in a swirl of life memories, as I was when I nearly drowned as a boy.

I know the truth of what I have just been told. In the presence of Death, I think of all my unfinished business, of things I need to do, of promises not yet fulfilled, of people I love. I have told myself many times that I am ready to die any day, but tonight a protest rises within me. I am ready to go, but not yet.

I don't plead, or rage, or try to make a deal. I just go over in my mind the things I will do if I have more time. I'll make more time for family, for swimming, for loving. I'll mend fences, make amends. I'll do more as a teacher and healer, as best I can, for those I can help and inspire.

These calculations are met with supreme indifference.

I'll create. I'll bring new things into the world. I'll tell better stories, and write them so more people will be encouraged to find their own bigger stories, and live those stories.

I feel an inner void. Has my visitor — I don't want to name him right now — gone away?

There is a constriction in my throat. I am naked under the sheet, but it feels exactly as if a necktie — or a noose — is being tightened.

The time of your death is now.

He does not show himself. The pressure on my neck is slowly released. Ah, it's not so hard to leave this body. My head, which I had raised against the pillows, droops over my chest. This is going to be so easy. I feel a tremendous need to rest, to sleep. I am letting myself go, not just the Traveler in me but all of me. It is done.

I raise up the body in the bed. The I that is speaking now is not identical to the one that just left, but indistinguishable from others and so very like my previous self that I don't need to make out that I have changed. I died and came back, in a moment. And my world split. Another me, on a parallel road in the many worlds, has joined the countless selves that have died already. I wonder whether he has gone to that wonderful penthouse apartment in the scholar city that my traveling self loves to visit.

Dawn is breaking over the Pic St. Loup. It brings out the warmth in the red-tiled roof that slopes down below my balcony. The boars are still quiet.

The time of your death is now.

What's this? It's not over?

However, the sentence is suspended for now, pending further review. You know what you must do.

I go to the desk, pick up my fountain pen, and start writing, in my leather-bound journal, a story that I hope will entertain Death.

About the Author

Robert Moss has been a dream traveler since doctors pronounced him clinically dead in a hospital in Hobart, Tasmania, when he was three years old. From his experiences in many worlds, he created his School of Active Dreaming, his original synthesis of modern dreamwork and ancient shamanic and mystical practices for journeying to realms beyond the physical. He leads popular workshops all over the world, including a three-year training for teachers of Active Dreaming and online courses for The Shift Network. A former lecturer in ancient history at the Australian National University, he is a *New York Times* bestselling novelist, poet, journalist, and independent scholar. His many books on dreaming, shamanism, and imagination include *Conscious Dreaming*, *The Secret History of Dreaming*, *Dreaming the Soul Back Home*, *The Boy Who Died and Came Back*, and *Sidewalk Oracles*. He has lived in upstate New York since he received a message from a red-tailed hawk under an old white oak.

His website is www.mossdreams.com.